PRAISE FOR *THE HIGHEST OF ALL MOUNTAINS*

"Pastor, peace practitioner, and scholar Samuel Sarpiya has given us more than another biblical basis of peacemaking book. *The Highest of All Mountains* brings biblical narratives into creative and constructive engagement with the lived stories of peacebuilding and conflict transformation embodied in Sarpiya's church and city. The linking of radical hospitality and the Jesus path to peace is especially instructive. As a Nigerian, South African, the author brings intercultural hermeneutics and his cosmopolitan affections together in an important theology of shalom."

—SCOTT HOLLAND
  Slabaugh Professor of Theology & Culture and Director of Peace Studies, Bethany Theological Seminary

"Peacemaking taken to another level while anchoring it in everyday life! *The Highest of All Mountains* is as timely as it is timeless. This may be one of the most visionary books written today that gives us a potential map for how we can individually and collectively navigate our way through a world where the marginalized continue to suffer from our structures and beliefs, towards a more intentionally beloved community where we work creatively to address injustice while compassionately uplifting each other. . . . This should be read alongside Dr. Martin Luther King's *Strength to Love* and Gene Sharp's *How Nonviolent Struggle Works*."

—NICHOLAS PATLER
  author of *Jim Crow and the Wilson Administration: Protesting Federal Segregation in the Early Twentieth Century*

"If you are awakening to the journey of peacemaking, nonviolence, and conflict transformation in the way of Jesus please get this book! Samuel Sarpiya is a practical, insightful, and trustworthy guide who helps us see our capacity for participating in the transformation of our neighborhoods. The stories in this book unveil faithful, healthy, and effective ways to disrupt the cycles of violence that plague our society."

—DREW HART

Assistant Professor of Theology, Messiah University, and author of *Who Will Be A Witness?: Igniting Activism for God's Justice, Love, and Deliverance*

"Peacemaking is at the center of belief and practice as Jesus followers. The way towards transformation of communities is through recognition of where there is conflict, unsustainable structures, and personal prideful bias. Samuel has offered wise and insightful correlations of research, historical storytelling, and personal lived experiences within communities where reform has taken place that has led to peacemaking. The questions at the end of each chapter offer opportunities to engage in the next step that is needed individually to take part in reconciliation work in relationships and communities. This work of peacemaking is essential to caring for one another in a compassionate way."

—JULIA HURLOW

Director of Discipleship, Taylor University

"Current global realties have brought to surface national issues worthy of discerning evaluation and transformation. Dr. Sarpiya's prophetic work invites us to radical hospitality practices among 'the feared' and creativity in areas our assumptions could leave us blinded to. If embodied, his insights could shift the trajectory of aspects of our culture from death to Life. . . . Do yourself and your neighbor a favor, read and enact these words. Bear witness then to Christ's love; heal the unalterably broken."

—HANS OINES

Christian missionary, Youth with A Mission (YWAM)

"As a peace practitioner for over twenty years, I only wish this book had been written over twenty years ago! It is amazingly balanced in its approach to peace and healing. It is immensely practical. It is also very biblical and historically orthodox."

—KAYODE BOLAJI

Executive Director, Peace Building Development Foundation, Nigeria

"*The Highest of All Mountains* presents revealing insights into man's understanding of conflict and his approach to resolving it. But, in lucid details, the author exposes man's inherent weakness and lack of capacity to deal with it in a selfless, sacrificial manner. Showing us the way out, the author takes the reader to passages in the Bible and points at the life of Jesus of Nazareth which, according to him, exemplifies the highest ethos in man's search for peaceful co-existence."

—JOHN TSOK

lawyer, Jos, Nigeria

"Dr. Sarpiya's book comes against the backdrop of continuous racial tensions in the part of the world he has chosen to live in. But the theme he explores resonates with other climates across the world. Whether it is the rude awakening in Jos, central Nigeria, the delicate reconciliation process in South Africa, or his community engagements in Rockford, USA, the book acknowledges the terrible strain on intercommunal relations. And when he takes the reader through very difficult moments that make peaceful coexistence a distant possibility, he also provides biblical precepts that can be employed to deal with obstacles to achieving it. A compelling read, this book points the way to peace and reconciliation in a world that needs it."

—Wulime Goyit

media professional, Jos, Nigeria

"In this book, Dr. Sarpiya describes in a sober and effective way how conflicts, either coming from racism, religious or social roots, can affect communities and whole nations in ways that divide populations into impassable trenches. . . . The author demonstrates with care how conflict transformation and peacemaking can, by the grace of God, be an efficient solution to ending years of mistrust and conflict between the different layers of society. . . . This is a book for those who believe that significant changes can be operated in a community by working and pursuing peace as it was thought by the Prince of Peace, Jesus Christ, as he taught it in his Sermon on the Mount."

—Eric Leblanc

pastor, Cowansville Connection Church, Quebec, Canada

The Highest of All Mountains

The Highest of All Mountains

A Guide for Christians Seeking Peace and Becoming Peacemakers

SAMUEL K. SARPIYA
foreword by Leonard Sweet
preface by Roger S. Nam

WIPF & STOCK · Eugene, Oregon

THE HIGHEST OF ALL MOUNTAINS
A Guide for Christians Seeking Peace and Becoming Peacemakers

Copyright © 2021 Samuel K. Sarpiya. All rights reserved. Except for brief quotations in critical publications or reviews, no part of this book may be reproduced in any manner without prior written permission from the publisher. Write: Permissions, Wipf and Stock Publishers, 199 W. 8th Ave., Suite 3, Eugene, OR 97401.

Wipf & Stock
An Imprint of Wipf and Stock Publishers
199 W. 8th Ave., Suite 3
Eugene, OR 97401

www.wipfandstock.com

PAPERBACK ISBN: 978-1-7252-7027-5
HARDCOVER ISBN: 978-1-7252-7026-8
EBOOK ISBN: 978-1-7252-7028-2

03/15/21

In the last days the mountain of the LORD's temple will be established as the highest of the mountains; it will be exalted above the hills, and all nations will stream to it.

   ISAIAH 2:2 *(NIV)*

Contents

Foreword by Leonard Sweet   xiii
Preface by Roger S. Nam   xv
Acknowledgments   xvii
Introduction   xix

PART I | THE THREE CONVERSIONS OF PETER: THE DISCIPLE'S CONVERSION TO PEACEMAKING

1   The Last Healing: Our Peace Is Mutual, for to Witness Healing Is to Be Healed   5
2   Put Down Your Sword: Jesus' Final Commandment Directs Us Towards Peace   13
3   To Come without Objection: Radical Hospitality Is Necessary for Multicultural Peacemaking   25

PART II | TO BE CONSCIOUS OF OUR SIN: THE COMMANDMENTS AND PATHWAYS OF PEACE

4   Eye for an Eye, Tooth for a Tooth: Old Testament Law in a New Testament World   39
5   Rain Falls on the Just and the Unjust: A Vision for Peace After the Covid-19 Plague   52
6   Tables in the Temple: Is There Such a Thing as Righteous Violence?   68

CONTENTS

PART III | THE HIGHEST PLACE: THE VISION OF THE PROMISED LAND

7	The Highest Place: Faith in Metaphor and in Action	81
8	Swords into Plowshares: Tools for Violence and Tools of Peace	89
9	I've Been to the Mountaintop: Beginning the Mission Together	103

Postscript   119
Bibliography   121
Index   135

Foreword

At the height of the Civil War in Ireland, "peace walls" were constructed in various cities to keep Protestants away from Catholics, and vice versa. Belfast alone was the scene of over 100 peace walls. Today these peace walls are a tourist attraction, having been turned into vast murals and other public art projects. But isn't the very phrase "peace wall" an oxymoron? How can peace divide us? Will our economic, political, religious, and civil divides ever be bridged by walls?

From the particularity of a mid-size American city, Dr. Samuel K. Sarpiya has written a personal account of how walls can become welcome mats and bistros can be made out of barricades. Arguably, two of the most shocking teachings of the founder of Christianity were these: the notion of loving one's enemies, and the stance of nonviolence. But as *The Highest of All Mountains* shows in one story after another, nonviolence is not an easy mountain to climb.

Pacifists is to imagine humans do not like war, and do not want war. The truth is war has many attractions, and these attractions outweigh the repulsions. At the deepest levels of the human heart, where sin and brokenness reside, we actually like war and want war.

1. We like the adventure of war—it inspires some of our greatest feats of daring and heroism.
2. We like the unity and community of war—the camaraderie it brings, the singleness of purpose, the intense focus, the need to be needed, to do our bit for a cause.

3. We like being caught up in a larger story—the drama of the whole, the righteousness of being right. There is no bit part in this story.
4. We like having our personal problems shrunk to the point where our problems pale to this life-or-death confrontation.
5. We like being angry and aggressive, and war channels our rage and vindicates our vindictiveness. You can only turn the cheek for so long without repressing a lot of unsanctified, uncivilized impulses.

The beauty and brilliance of this book is it shows how the satisfactions and attractions of peace are greater than those of war. War demands heroism, but peace compels even greater heroism than does war. You will come away from this book with a renewed sense that Jesus was right: the power of force is a farce, and there is no peace so enduring, so exhilarating, so balmy, even so barmy at times, as the peace you keep in Christ. When ancient Christian burial grounds, like those in the catacombs of Rome, carried the inscription that someone died "in pace" or "in peace," it means Christ's peace, not the world's peace. And the peace that passes all understanding, the perfect peace that only Christ can give, is a peace where RIP means not the world's "Rest in Peace" but the church's "Rise in Power."

LEONARD SWEET, author (*Rings of Fire*), professor (George Fox University, Drew University, Tabor College, Evangelical Seminary), and founder of preachthestory.com and The Salish Sea Press.

Preface

For many years, Dr. Samuel Sarpiya has been paving the way of forgiveness and peace.

The following pages narrate moments of Dr. Sarpiya's story as an interpretive frame for Scripture and the fecund result of a lifelong approach to peacemaking. He grew up in Jos, Nigeria, a community that witnessed violent conflict between Muslim and Christian communities. From youth, Dr. Sarpiya was identified as a rising leader in a local Christian Boy's Brigade.

But Dr. Sarpiya learned to reject the expectations of violent defense of faith traditions. Instead, Dr. Sarpiya was compelled to follow a life of peaceful reconciliation as the best reflection of the Great Commission. He has worked with the Nigerian Security Agencies to develop peaceful strategies in engagement with Boko Haram. He served in Amsterdam by promoting reconciliation with trafficked African immigrants. For over a decade, he was a resource in championing nonviolence in Rockford, Illinois, one of the most religiously diverse cities in the United States. His journey has taken him to Cape Town, as he tirelessly works against the deleterious legacies of apartheid. He does not present himself as a larger-than-life prophet rescuer. He would self-describe as a just a man, like anyone else, yet with a deep commitment to the process of peacebuilding.

In these pages, you will see the core of peacebuilding in the most vulnerable spaces, such as when the family shop is in the midst of Muslim-Christian violence in Jos, and seeing other children end up with limbs missing or even dead. In another section, Dr. Sarpiya recounts his adrenaline skyrocketing when being pulled over by the police in Rockford, where Africanness blended with African American realities. In the midst of these harrowing accounts, Dr. Sarpiya also recalls the interventions of key individuals, who nurtured a penchant towards nonviolence. Often these individuals were outside of the Christian tradition, such as a particularly influential Sufi hermit. But despite their religious differences, Dr. Sarpiya gravitated towards the shared commitment of nonviolence.

These experiences frame Dr. Sarpiya's interpretation of biblical texts. He faithfully embraces the totality of Scripture through this lens of reconciliation. As expected, he engages with passages on Jesus' healing of the ear and the admonition to turns swords into plowshares. But at the same time, Dr. Sarpiya also reflects on Jesus' violent overturning of the money-changers' tables. Sarpiya reads these texts courageously and reflectively. He skillfully honors the theological tension and the peculiarities of the historical context. His hermeneutical approach will inspire.

This book gives an opportunity for a wider audience to walk alongside Dr. Sarpiya and better understand this frame for interpreting biblical texts towards a deeply rooted value of peacebuilding. For Dr. Sarpiya, the book is an invitation to learn to be a peacemaker. The words are less preachy, and more like those of a storyteller. I encourage you to read reflectively. Pause as the stories. Pray through the Scriptures and imagine hearing the voice of Dr. Sarpiya, who has devoted himself to peacebuilding across multiple continents. Use the questions as opportunities for inward exploration. The work of peacebuilding call.

ROGER NAM

Acknowledgments

I would like to acknowledge the support and hard work of Gimbiya Kettering, my friend and primary go-to for conversation about how things are shaping up, who not only helped me shape the overall structure of this book but also helped me rearrange the content, pushing me to engage with practical ideas as I sought to improve the quality of my work. I also want to thank Wipf & Stock editors for their support and for taking a risk on a novice writer like me; their trust in me is greatly appreciated. I would like to acknowledge Roger Nam for his continued support for Portland Seminary and now Emory University, for allowing me the access to research and to write during board of regent meetings and at other times. I would like to thank YWAM Dunham, the base leadership, who gave me the freedom to pursue this dream of writing with much support. Thank you to Portland Seminary Faculty, Loren and Cliff, and most especially Len Sweet, who has given himself to be present when I needed him to preach at our denominational conference. Thank you to brother Danyaro Sarpiya, who really went out of his way financially to help make graduate school a possibility and to make my passion for ministry possible. And most especially, thanks to Gretchen, my friend, companion, and wonderful mother to our three daughters—Anna, Ella-Joy, and Deborah (Bo)—who kept everyone on task while I was traveling, researching, and engaging in ministry adventures. She makes all this possible and is always asking "How is the reading and writing coming?" Gretchen believed in this work even when I did not. I love you.

Introduction

The world we live in is full of violence and stressful events. So much of this violence is caused when people are not able to resist acting on their thoughts, feelings, and actions, and cannot recognize their human weakness. Thus, violence can also arise from some weak interpersonal relationships in a family or community when individuals experience an inability to communicate carefully and effectively with each other. Religious communities present a particular challenge, because embedded in religion is a dual, complex legacy with regard to peace and violence.

Conflict transformation practitioners must therefore be more systematic in implementing strategies, if meaningful transformation is to be useful in certain contexts. However, "policymakers, diplomats, journalists, and scholars who are ready to over-interpret economic causality are still in the habit of disregarding the role of religion, religious institutions, and religious motivations in explaining politics and conflict."[1] This book hopes to stimulate dialogue in the area of active nonviolence and conflict transformation principles and practices, and most especially as it relates to religious communities.

My use of stories from practical experience from a mid-size American city is an attempt to stimulate dialogue among young and old, religious and the not-so-religious, and interreligious dialogues with people caught in the crossfire of violence, thereby missing

1. Johnston and Sampson, *Religion*, 8.

Introduction

their potential to make peace and transform the ensuing conflict. In doing so, this book will show evidence from scholarly research as well as success stories, documented with particular attention that is duplicable in different cities in America and around the globe.

This book tells the story of growing a multicultural congregation that is rooted in Christ's teachings of peace and reconciliation. I also share the implications of what it means to be a congregation that is part of a historic peace denomination, but one that is unique, as most members were raised in other traditions. So, together we are redefining pacifism for a mid-size city, inner-city, and even a rural context, and leading conversations about peacemaking that go beyond tradition and heritage into direct, practical action.

My work as a peacemaker "requires the strengthening of spiritual lives by prayer, Bible study, and worship in order to connect with Christ, the giver of peace, realizing that apart from Christ we can do nothing."[2] We are called to love our neighbor(s) and our neighbor(s) may be from a different religious tradition, recognizing that difference and yet giving them their needed space for the sake of unity, not uniformity.

This book narrates stories from my experiences of active peacemaking as a pastor and researcher, impacted by Jesus' teaching on nonviolence and peace, living out a pastoral presence in my community within the area school system, and equipping and training the local police department's command staff and management in nonviolent principles of community policing.

This book is for people who believe the gospel is a message of peace, and this gospel of peace is relevant for our time. Peacemaking is a core part of our Christian discipleship. Just as we learn how to pray, to accept God's grace, to love our neighbors, and to feed the hungry, we can also learn how to be peacemakers. I believe peacemaking is central to Christian faith and practice.

I am writing this book to serve as a guide that would offer a scriptural basis with practical stories and applications. Because I'm challenged by Scriptures, I wanted to write a guide that includes

---

2. Segler and Bradley, *Christian Worship*, 4.

the contemporary and real-life application of the biblical vision to peacemaking in action.

The stories in this book are full of constructive spiritual and social change for anyone seeking ways to engage their communities in difficult conversations about race, socioeconomics, our broken justice system, religious differences, and seeking the common good for all.

When people hear stories from communities that are ending violence, building relationships, and creating a lasting peace, we often think it's too hard. It's impossible here, now, in our places. Or we think we couldn't do that. We're not important enough, we don't have skills, we are waiting for someone else to be a peacemaker. I'm writing this book to remind everyone, even myself, that it is possible and each of us has the gifts, talents, and faith to be a part of God's good news and God's plan for peace with a purpose to;

- Invite and enhance active Christian commitment to non-violence and conflict transformation;
- promote peace between opposing religions;
- stimulate open and honest conversation among communities that could lead to radical commitment to peacemaking, and;
- develop leaders with an ability to listen to each other, even in opposing-view situations.

PART I

The Three Conversions of Peter
The Disciple's Conversion to Peacemaking

And I tell you, you are Peter, and on this rock, I will build my church, and the gates of hell shall not prevail against it.
   MATTHEW 16:18

CHAPTER 1: THE LAST HEALING: OUR PEACE IS MUTUAL, FOR TO WITNESS HEALING IS TO BE HEALED

Objective: Peacemaking is CORE to Jesus' Message and the Gospel

In the Garden of Gethsemane, when the guards come to take Jesus, Peter slices off a man's ear to protect and defend his Savior. Armed and zealous, Peter thinks his righteous anger is justice. But Jesus, the Savior of the world, heals the man, and in doing so, shows Peter another way: the way of forgiveness and peace. Peter's actions in this story are somewhat similar to a personal experience of witnessing the healing of Haruna and myself, our journey from acting as Peter in to becoming peacemakers.

CHAPTER 2: PUT DOWN YOUR SWORD: JESUS' FINAL COMMANDMENT DIRECTS US TOWARDS PEACE

Objective: Applying for Today What It Means for Disciples to Put Away the Sword

The last recorded teaching of Jesus to his disciples is to put away their swords. The evening that Christ is being arrested, falsely convicted, and sentenced to death seems like the wrong time for a message of peace. Yet, for the Christian peacemaker, such times are the most important. For me, it is when a White police officer pulls me over, turning a traffic infraction into a life-or-death moment, that I realize I have held a sword of judgment against African Americans. It is the same racialized judgment held against me and it is in that moment that I can put it down to really become an advocate for interracial peacemaking.

Part I | The Three Conversions of Peter

CHAPTER 3: TO COME WITHOUT OBJECTION: RADICAL HOSPITALITY IS NECESSARY FOR MULTICULTURAL PEACEMAKING

Objective: Radical Peacemaking Is a Radical Hospitality of Refreshment and Refugee

Too often, invitations to friends and colleagues are superficial and polite. It is easier to meet people for coffee than invite them into our homes. Even in our homes, it is difficult to open ourselves up beyond the house tour. Christian hospitality, drawing on the message of Christ and Hebrew traditions, is intended to be untamed, sacrificial, and to ultimately set aside the cultural differences of the world. The model of Peter and Cornelius reminds us how kindness and empathy lead to peace.

1

The Last Healing

Our Peace Is Mutual, for to Witness Healing Is to Be Healed

"But Jesus answered, "No more of this." And He touched the man's ear and healed him.

LUKE 22:47–52

"Nonviolence is a powerful and just weapon, which cuts without wounding and ennobles the man who wields it. It is a sword that heals."[1]

MARTIN LUTHER KING JR.

---

1. King, "Nobel Lecture," para. 16.

Part I | The Three Conversions of Peter

PEACEMAKING AS CORE TO JESUS' MESSAGE

I am now in Gethsemane. Like the garden outside the city of Jerusalem, I return to it again and again. It is a place to be curious, to ask all kinds of questions from the day's events, a place where you make confession, confessing all the wrongs you have committed during the day, and most especially when you fail to understand Jesus' teachings. But it is also a place where your doubts are met with some reassurance of grace and peace.

My first time at the garden was as a young member of the Boys Brigade (similar to how an American boy between the ages of 11 and 18 might join the Boys Scouts). In Jos, we join the Boys Brigade, a youth group that seeks to defend Christian causes, although outsiders view this group as a Christian militia simply because of their teachings on self-defense and the defense of the Christian faith. Christians, on the other hand, see it as a noble cause because of the spiritual content that is lacking in the Boy Scouts, which is considered a secular organization.

When I was younger, I thought there were only two ways to the garden of Gethsemane: to come as Peter did (who came in with Jesus and with his sword hidden), or as Malchus did, (sword drawn and ready for a fight).

The first time I was there I was waiting to pick up my sword to defend the Christian cause for my community against Muslim uprisings, which were beginning to be a frequent occurrence.

I was born in Jos to a Christian family, a minority group in my community. Jos is city of about 900,000 in northern Nigeria, a tourist city but with a boomtown-like mentality due to the discovery of mineral resources, which led to a mining boom in the 1950s. Jos is also the administrative, commercial, and tourist capital of Plateau State, and can be described as the fault line between the predominantly Muslim north and the predominantly Christian south of Nigeria, often referred to as the middle belt.

The road to leadership was mapped out for me when, as a teenager, I joined the Boys Brigade group that seeks to defend the Christian cause in this predominantly Muslim region. I was mentored by their general secretary, who envisioned that I would one day become a group leader, so he helped lay the groundwork for what would be my future service to the Boys Brigade.

However, Nigeria has been and continues to be impacted greatly by religious violence, with fighting between Muslims and Christians occurring frequently. During one of the skirmishes that reached my neighborhood, I was encouraged by this leader to join the other young men on the frontlines. Biblical Scriptures have been used in many places as a justification for violence. We were taught that God had used military force to defend God's children, the Israelites, and that we were God's children now. As we stood side by side in our uniforms, listening to instructions, the general secretary reminded us that as Israelites went to war for saving their people, so we were now doing the same.

In 1983, the fight became personal for me when a conflict broke out between the majority-Muslim and minority-Christian populations over control of the weekly market square in my community, where my mom had a store. Being the minority and thus outnumbered, more than twenty Christians were killed. These included my friends, but the luckier ones—those who survived the frontlines—woke up to find arms and legs missing, severed by machetes. None of their lives would be the same.

While all this was taking place in my own neighborhood, I became acquainted with a Muslim youth named Haruna, who was my age. We shared meals together at the same boarding school but didn't know each other that well. By this time, I was committed to the Boys' Brigade, and he to the Muslim equivalent. Just as I was taught to be a leader who will willingly die to protect my Christian faith and community, he was also envisioned as a leader who would willingly die to protect his Muslim community. We were being taught from our respective books—the Bible and the Qu'ran—the theologies we would need both for intellectual discourse and also to prepare our hearts for violence.

But in the midst of this was a rising Sufi hermit, a different type of Muslim, a different reading from the Qu'ran, and he was drawing a large group of Muslim youth to himself because of his focus on another way of being Muslim. Sufism choses a mystical form of Islam, a school of practice that emphasizes the inward search for God and shuns materialism. Its modern-day adherents cherish tolerance and pluralism, qualities that in many religions unsettle extremists. Haruna was mentored by Sheikh Danjuma, the Sufi hermit, but there were so many other voices. As the Sheik tried to guide Haruna from any act of senseless violence, the wider culture was pushing Haruna and myself towards a clash.

It was a message Haruna finally understood too late. It was only after the Christian militia men, my people, killed Haruna's mentor and threw his body down a well that Haruna's mission became one of revenge—one his mentor would not have wanted. Haruna swore he would kill any and every Christian he came across. Then, one Friday afternoon sermon during a Muslim worship service, in the sermon, Haruna's imam told the story of the prophet Muhammad, "who had gone to preach at Ta'if, a town about seventy miles southeast of Mecca. Bleeding after being stoned and cast outside the city,"[2] Muhammad "was visited by an angel who asked, if he would like those who mistreated him to be destroyed. Muhammad said no."[3] Haruna felt the imam was talking directly to him during the sermon. The next time Haruna and I met, Haruna, in tears, reported he had forgiven the Christian militia that killed his mentor. To prove his commitment to this new way of life, he went to visit the sick and the wounded in the nearby Christian neighborhood. Over time, Haruna and I have developed a stronger bond of friendship that goes beyond our religious differences. Haruna and I have a passion for peace, justice, and reconciliation.

Even as friends, we both quietly longed for the other to be converted to our faith and way of life. I wanted Haruna to experience what I had experienced in Gethsemane, where my doubts and fears were answered by Jesus. Given the wider culture, where religious violence is becoming prevalent, encountering Jesus' message of peace meant everything to me.

Just as Haruna was finding inspiration in the teachings of a Sufi hermit, I was gaining a renewed understanding of the gospel as a message of peace. So, I wanted Haruna to experience what

---

2. Emerick, *Life and Work of Muhammad*, 32.
3. Emerick, *Life and Work of Muhammad*, 255.

The Last Healing

following Jesus looks and feels like, but I could sense Haruna wanted me to experience his Islamic faith as well. In spite of that, we remained friends and continued to work toward peace, justice, and reconciliation for all, irrespective of religious affiliation. This journey has left me convinced that peacemaking and evangelism are not mutually exclusive, because this violence was not going to solve anything.

Just as it happened in the garden, when Malchus's ear was healed by Jesus, my relationship with Haruna is the modern Gethsemane story. Now I believe there are two ways to come into the garden: you can either come with Jesus or you can come with the soldiers to arrest Jesus. There are also two ways to depart the garden: you can depart as Malchus did, having entered with the sword drawn but left after experiencing the healing of Jesus, or you can enter with Jesus like Peter did, still carrying your sword, ready to use it, and leave ready to deny Jesus like Peter did three times.

The contemporary expression of the garden for me is that of living in North America, as it would be hard to escape conversations about race, racism, and violence. Followers of Jesus have no option but to engage in a meaningful way in the hope of demonstrating that the teachings of Jesus are centered around viewing the gospel as a message of peace. Christians' only option is to engage biblically in an attempt to deal directly and honestly with these very difficult issues. I am aware there may be some who sincerely believe violence and racism have long since been removed from our civic or church denominational life. And there are others who believe it to be rare and isolated, despite seeing it flashing daily in the news and sometimes people even attributing that to "fake news." I am in no way doubting that sincere people can have such assumptions, but I do however believe they may not be looking at things objectively. The most fundamental reason for this is because violence and racism are, at their very core, spiritual sicknesses. They are sins, and sin is never far from us.

The story of the first sin, Adam and Eve, reminds us we are all descendants of the first parents. Every human being, regardless of race and nationality, are made in the image of God. Racism and other manifestations of injustice are not merely the result of

Part I | The Three Conversions of Peter

historical forces, economic interests, or lack of education alone—they are a denial of the God in each of us. It is a symptom that takes it next step with the biblical account of the brothers Cain and Abel, moving from sin to violence. And if we are going to change our biblical worldview, we must first affirm the unity of the human race and recognize that violence only pits brother against brother.

In every generation, if we don't want to repeat the mistakes of the previous generation, then we need to be clear about the message of the gospel, the good news, the announcement that the saving work of Jesus Christ to all who believe in him is a message of healing, it is forgiveness from sin, it is hope for eternal life. But it is also, at its core, the embodiment of the message of peace. When Jesus heals Malchus in Gethsemane, he is bringing healing to his enemy who is also his neighbor. As Christians, we are to be motivated by the fact that we can heal. Healing is transformation love made visible.

PEACE AS HEALING, MIRACULOUS

The garden of Gethsemane is said to be within a few hundred steps of Jerusalem's gate. This garden emerges from the narrow streets along with closely clustered residences. In the silence of the night, it feels as much withdrawn from the world as if in a wilderness.

Jesus often retired from the crowds to Gethsemane. The depressive politics or the stresses of life can drive any of us crazy looking for a silent place; for Jesus, it was Gethsemane. Scriptures tell us he often retired there and he was able to better converse with his chosen disciples and to answer their questions. The disciples often came to him with questions and their anxieties and fears; it was there that he could calm them.

Gethsemane also served as a place of preparation for the trials that lay ahead. If they were not in the upper room, Bethany, then they could be found at Gethsemane. And because Judas had often been there with the rest, and had been witness to the kind of piety, wisdom, sympathy, and tenderness of Jesus while in the place of prayer, he must have concluded such would be a good place to strike.

THE LAST HEALING

The events that occurred in the garden of Gethsemane the night before the crucifixion have continued to reverberate throughout the corridors of history to this day. The story of what took place in Gethsemane was so transformational that all four gospels include the extraordinary story of this event. To recount, Jesus and his disciples had just celebrated the feast of the Passover. They then went to the garden. While in the garden, Jesus at one point took three out of the disciples that were with him—Peter, James, and John—further while the others waited. While separated from the rest, Jesus asked them to watch with him and pray so they would not fall into temptation. But the long week and most especially the long tiring day got the best of them and they could not stay awake.

Jesus had to wake them twice and remind them to pray so they too would not fall into temptation. This was especially heart-breaking because Peter did eventually fall into temptation that very night. First, he took out his sword to defend Jesus against his captors, and later, three times he denied even knowing Jesus. John 18:25-27 says, "Now Simon Peter stood and warmed himself. Therefore, they said to him, 'You are not also one of His disciples, are you?' He denied it and said, 'I am not!' One of the servants of the high priest, a relative of him whose ear Peter cut off, said, 'Did I not see you in the garden with Him?' Peter then denied again, and immediately a rooster crowed."

Soon after they have finished praying, Judas Iscariot, the betrayer, arrived with a crowd of people that involved soldiers, high priests, Pharisees, and their servants to arrest Jesus. In a moving emotional gesture, Judas identified Jesus by a prearranged signal he had given them, that is, a kiss.

What followed is not quite clear; we tend to conflate or blend the four gospel accounts into one narrative. The accounts in the four gospels differ. Mark's Gospel says a bystander cut off the ear of the high priest's servant (14:47), which still proves there was no protest on the part of Jesus. Matthew's account says the ear was cut off by "one of the disciples," that is, one of those who were with Jesus, but Jesus rebuked him, saying, "Put your sword back into its place" (Matt 26:52). Luke reports that the incident began with a question put to Jesus, "Lord should we strike with the sword?" (22:49), and as *one of them* struck the right ear of the high priest's servant, Jesus says, "No more of this" (22:51). John's Gospel identifies Simon Peter and the servant named Malchus, whereupon Jesus rebuked Peter, "Put your sword back into its sheath" (18:11).

I take the liberty to go with John's narrative of Peter's act of fierce loyalty to his master. Taking matters to heart, Peter attacked and cut off an ear of Malchus, the high priest's bodyguard. But Jesus rebuked Peter, and even went ahead to miraculously heal the man's ear. By this unexpected show of goodwill, Jesus demonstrates that the aggressor is worthy of healing. This strange event in the garden of Gethsemane brings to the fore Jesus' views of violence. What are we to do with Jesus' words? Many justifications are advanced for retaliation, but according to Jesus, he forgives you even when you are in the Boys Brigade, acting against his will. Even then, he still loves you. Such a forgiveness calls us first to God, but it is also important the such a call rekindles an awareness of our divine vocation, which we often take for granted in the midst of our many daily responsibilities. As Jesus says, "You did not choose me, but I chose you" (John 15:16). This means returning to the source of our calling. Malchus left Gethsemane, having experienced the healing work of Christ, and as a result he will always be a witness to the account of the miracles afforded to him. Have you experienced a miracle?

QUESTIONS FOR REFLECTION:

- Identify someone with whom you'd like to become closer. It could be someone you know well or someone you're just getting to know. Can you recognize yourself as the aggressor Malchus or Peter?
- What does friendship mean to you?
- How do you think Jesus would respond to your previous answer in relation to the Scriptures about the gospel as a message of peace?
- What does healing mean to you? When have you received healing you did not deserve? Or what do you long to be healed of, even though you might be the one who started the aggression?

2

Put Down Your Sword

Jesus' Final Commandment Directs Us Towards Peace

"Do you think I cannot call on My Father, and he will at once put at my disposal more than twelve legions of angels?"

MATTHEW 26:53

"The hunger for love is much more difficult to remove than the hunger for bread."[1]

MOTHER TERESA

---

1. Mother Teresa, *In the Heart of the World*, 12.

Part I | The Three Conversions of Peter

PEACE IN THE MIDST OF ONGOING CONFLICT: PETER AND CORNELIUS

It is easy to forget that early messianic movements were looking for a militant overthrow of Roman rule. The most faithful, religious people believed they needed to be a part of a local armed-and-ready militia. They followed conspiracy theories about the leaders, and claimed righteousness based on their purity. But Christianity was, from the earliest days, different. Jesus taught that the paths of the zealots, those engaged in armed revolt against Rome, were going to begin and end by the sword. Instead, he offered a way of life in forgiveness, justice, and peace. Christians took to heart Jesus' teaching and instead of the paths of the zealots they continually live and teach the message as taught by Jesus.

Peter, as the unofficial leader of the apostles and founder of the church, came from a Zealot background. He was ready for the overthrow of Rome and believed his commitment was so pure he would never deny Jesus. This was akin to a pledge of allegiance for Peter, to defend his Lord and Master. He is ready to be killed. Peter is a loyalist to the core.

Peter, sword in his robe, is the opposite of what Christ preached. To be a follower of Jesus, we are called and are expected to follow the path of peace, not war. It is in following that path of peace that we would be called children of God: "blessed are the peacemakers for they shall be the children of God" (Matt 5:9, paraphrase). Nonetheless, many today suggest such act of peacemaking is not what we are expected to do and to be; we are expected to fight back. Such belief expects a sense of self-defense, with a "fight back" attitude. It was as if Peter never listened to Jesus, the Prince of Peace.

It should be clear Jesus objected to the use of the sword. He was quite clear that those who use such weapons for the sake of self-defense would find that ineffective, for violence begets violence. Those who engage in glorifying that shall find such violence kills them spiritually. Jesus did not want his disciples to take up literal weapons but rather to offer themselves as living sacrifices to God.

PUT DOWN YOUR SWORD

Peter insisted emphatically, "Even if I have to die with you, I will never disown you" (Matt 25:35). Peter, in his attempt to defend Jesus from the arresters, took out his sword, cutting the ear of a Roman soldier. He was then rebuked by Jesus and told to put down his sword. Peter still kept his commitment to following Jesus, which he did through following the arrest of Jesus by sneaking through the city as recorded in the Gospels, while the rest of the disciples fled for their lives.

Peter's action in the garden is sometimes dismissed as ridiculous, but he was sincere in his zealous following of Jesus. His action shows his resolve as someone determined to protect Jesus. But Jesus was on a mission to protect and restore humanity to their rightful relationship with God. In Gethsemane, he was preparing to go to the cross, offering up his life, and being arrested by the guards as a means of offering lasting peace amid an ongoing conflict.Something happened between the garden experience and the resurrection. Peter went through what I would call a second conversion, the first of which occurred when Jesus called him to, "Come follow me" (Matt 4:9). After spending over three years with Jesus as a zealot, Peter finally understood the message of forgiveness and healing, when he responded by putting down the sword, which led to a second conversion where Peter went from the sword-drawn disciple against a Roman soldier to a man responding to the call to engage with a Roman soldier, Cornelius. The pivotal moment came when Peter had a third conversion experience which was the radical racial awakening, in this third conversion it came in a dream of him going to eat with Cornelius.

We have to remember Peter lived all his life in a Jewish culture similar to white culture in America, enjoying any and every privilege that comes with being in with the culture. He had been taught it was a sin to eat with a gentile or even go into a gentile home. All of a sudden, in Acts 10, we meet a man named Cornelius, a God-fearing Roman who lived in Caesarea, a town on the coast of the Mediterranean Sea. Cornelius was a commander of about 100 soldiers and was a gentile who prayed to God and gave alms (a form of repentance among Jews), unlike most of the Roman soldiers who were steeped in idol worship. It was recorded that he

PART I | THE THREE CONVERSIONS OF PETER

prayed regularly to the one true God, and not only did he pray but he was involved in an act of offering hospitality to those in need around him. But Cornelius was also a gentile in the eyes of the Jews of his day.

Cornelius received a vision from the Lord during a time of prayer. In that vision the angel of the Lord said to him, "Your prayers and gifts have been received by the Lord as and offering" (Acts 10:31). He was then instructed to send men to Joppa to bring Simon Peter, and without missing a beat, Cornelius quickly did as he had been instructed in the vision. Meanwhile, Peter was in prayer as well on the rooftop at the house where he was staying in Joppa, when he suddenly had a vision telling him to eat meat that seemed unclean. Of course Peter rejected any idea of doing that, since he was a devout Jesus-follower and was not about to make himself unclean with food. Peter wrestled with what that entailed, the idea that the kingdom of God was being opened up to the gentile as well. This vision came to Peter three times, symbolic of him denying Jesus three times. By the end of the third vision, the servants of Cornelius had arrived to bring Peter back to Cornelius's house.

It would have been easy for Peter to distinguish himself as a part of an elite group. After all, he was one of the twelve disciples. It was to him that Jesus said, "Blessed are you, Simon son of Jonah, for this was not revealed to you by man, but by my Father in heaven. And I tell you that you are Peter, and on this rock I will build my church, and the gates of Hades will not overcome it. I will give you the keys of the kingdom of heaven; whatever you bind on earth will be bound in heaven, and whatever you loose on earth will be loosed in heaven" (Matt 16:17–19). It was Peter who preached the first sermon, who led literally thousands of converts to the new faith that one day would be known as Christianity (Acts 2). It was Peter whose very shadow, when cast on the sick, healed them (Acts 5).

Peter was particularly proud to have been of the Jewish faith and race. After all, Jesus had said, "Salvation comes from the Jews" (John 4:22). The Creator of all had come to earth as Messiah and had been born into a Jewish household and he was of the line of the great king of Israel, David. Peter took his faith seriously. Leviticus 11 forbade the observing Jew to eat "unclean animals" (v. 31), so he didn't do so. He wouldn't be caught dead in intimate fellowship with a gentile, though surely he remembered Jesus sitting at the well, talking to the Samaritan woman. A lot had happened to Peter in a relatively short period. He'd experienced the infilling of the Holy Spirit at Pentecost.

Three is something of a magical number for Peter: three times before the cock crowed he denied being one of the Twelve. It was about this time that *three* of Cornelius's servants showed up at the gate of Simon's home, asking about a man named Peter and whether or not he was staying there. Simultaneously, God's Spirit informed Peter that the men were there and that he should go with them back to the gentile's home.

Peter not only let go of his fishing net to follow Jesus, he put down his sword, but he also put down his Jewish identity. To put down your sword can be expressed in various ways. To some it would mean using their privilege to fight for justice; for others it may mean a total surrender and letting go of the status quo, that privileged position of power; and yet for others, it may mean letting go of stereotypes. But before that can happen, there has to be a realization that holding onto one's sword can lead to spiritual alienation from God's original call for us to be peacemakers.

My putting down my sword experience has occurred multiple times in my faith journey. First, beginning with becoming a Christian in Nigeria and with being taught to defend the Christian and realizing that is not a by-the-sword thing; then moving to South Africa at a time when South Africa was beginning to engage with other African countries in a new way, following the first democratic election post-apartheid, relating to the rest of Africa in a new way. In South Africa, I had to learn to put down my sword to become a bridge-builder peacemaker without taking sides in a nation that has been divided by race, putting down my sword by not taking sides with black South Africans but rather working intentionally to build relationships between the different racial groups.

As I moved to Hawaii, I had to put down another kind of sword in my discipleship journey. Hawaii is often described as a melting pot with not one particular ethnic group that comprises the majority of the population. In other words, everyone is a minority.

Part I | The Three Conversions of Peter

There is no other state in the United States where no one ethnic group or race represents the majority of people. Hawaii has the largest percentage of Asian Americans and multi-racial Americans. It also has the lowest percentage of Caucasians in the union. I find myself working for a mission organization that is supposed to be international, intercultural, and interdenominational, but yet in Hawaii, this mission organization is predominantly Caucasian (white North American). In that setting, I had to put down another sword of being a minority in a predominantly white mission organization in a multicultural society like Hawaii.

While in Hawaii, I lived on the Big Island, which is the common term used for the state of Hawaii. This island is growing by more than forty-two acres each year because of the Kilauea Volcano, which has been erupting for about thirty years now—an impressive feat. Mauna Loa is one of the biggest volcanoes in the entire world. It is also located on the Big Island and its lava fields were once a training site for astronauts before they went to the moon. This state is the only one in the US that grows coffee, vanilla beans, and cacao commercially. Hawaii's highest and lowest recorded temperatures have both occurred on the Big Island, which isn't very surprising because of this island's diverse landscape.[2]

Moving from a very close compound space in YWAM-Hawaii, to the Chicagoland part of the American heartland, I suddenly find myself living within the American racial hierarchy. Like most Africans whose perspective has been clouded by the precolonial ideal of divide and rule—kind of like Peter, who had the sword of cultural superiority—I realize I too have that sword and this sword comes from colonialism's influence. I am not scapegoating colonialism here but I had an attitude about Blackness and Black America that lack the history of slavery, racism, and the civil rights movement.

Moving to the Midwest, and Rockford, Illinois in particular, I was confronted with another sword that I had to put down. When I moved to Rockford, I intentionally planted a multiracial church, my goal was to make this racial diversity my mission, and in the

---

2. https://www.thefactsite.com/interesting-hawaii-facts/.

midst of that I was confronted with racism by a police officer, who pulled me over for driving 35mph in a 30mph zone. By ticketing me, as well as taking and keeping my driver's license instead of sending it to the appropriate office for processing, my Africanness became blended with my African American brothers and sisters, who often face predatory policing, one of the high prices of driving while black. Up to this point, I had operated under the assumption that such does not happen to folks like me from the motherland. However, for example, "A 2014 federal report found that St. Louis area police's use of traffic stops to raise revenue through fines was an underlying cause of racial unrest. For African Americans pulled over up to 10 times as often as white neighbor."[3] My African origin could not save me; I was just like any Black American. There wasn't any differentiation between me and my Black American brothers and sisters and my offense was driving while black.[4]

I was confronted with the sword of judgment that judges African Americans without considering the anthropological context of how and why things happen in their communities the way they do. This sort of thinking has led to an unintentional perception of African Americans by Africans in the diaspora; for example, people like me. We often ask how they can be in a country of plenty and remain mostly at the bottom of the socio-economic ladder, casting of aspersion on Black America without understanding the historical context, the role of slavery and Jim Crow laws played, or the years that followed, up through the Civil Rights movement. I had to learn what it means to put down my sword from the moment I realized I was judgmental of my African American sisters and brothers.

However, in contemporary African and African-American relationships, a lot has been said about these two groups in the United States. It is expected that since both are descendants from the same root culture, they will adapt and coexist in harmony. However, doubts have been raised about this coexistence and adaptation. The growing stereotypes, misconceptions, ignorance, grudges, and cultural differences are largely responsible for some of

3. Lartey, "Predatory Police," para. 1.
4. Lartey, "Predatory Police."

Part I | The Three Conversions of Peter

these strained relationships. Can anything explain this reality other than these elements?

Intellectuals like Martin Delany, Paul Hopkins, W. E. B. Du Bois, Marcus Garvey, and Tiemako Garan Kouyaté have engaged in and devoted time in their studies to the importance of understanding of Africans, African Americans, Afro-Caribbean blacks, and blacks elsewhere. According to Brent Hayes Edward, the term "African Diaspora" is often used to "express the links and commonalities among groups of African descent throughout the world."[5]

The African diaspora in the Americas started in the seventeenth century during the trans-Atlantic slave trade. After the end of the trans-Atlantic slave trade, some freed slaves repatriated to Africa; however, many stayed and endured social, political, and economic marginalization. Those freed slaves who stayed were given labels from "Negro" to "Black" to "African American." It is widely believed that African Americans are also part of the African diaspora. As Copeland-Carson noted, "Pan-Africanist scholars as early as Du Bois attempted to define the diaspora as a model for African and African American cultural dynamics. This earlier conception of the African diaspora conceived of it as the cultural aggregate of individuals of African descent."[6]

As an African in diaspora, the realization that I have to be decolonized of the colonial view of my perspective of African American as opposed to Africans in what we call the motherland is a sword I continue to wrestle with, hoping and praying I can always remember that, like Peter, carrying that sword into the garden would not be of any use, since I have Jesus.

Accordingly, Kwadwo Konadu-Agyemang and Baffour K. Takyi give a considerable historical explanation to the African diaspora by stressing that "the immigration of Africans to the North American continent is not a new phenomenon. Indeed, the African presence in this region goes back further, and may predate the era of

---

5. Edwards, "Uses of 'Diaspora,'" 3.
6. Copeland-Carson, *Creating Africa in America*, 19.

PUT DOWN YOUR SWORD

the infamous slave trade when significant numbers of West African slaves were brought to the colonies of the New world."[7]

The United States's immigration policy has also been very helpful. This view is coherent with Diana Baird N'Diaye's. She states:

> "Since the 1960s, several complex circumstances have contributed to attracting increased immigration and transnational activity of Africans to the United States. Some of these factors, both political and economic, include the decline of European colonization and economic influence in Africa, the concurrent growth of United States participation in Africa affairs, changes in US immigration laws, and the existence of an established African American population"[8]

One burning issue that seems to pull apart African immigrants and African Americans is ignorance about each other's culture and past. These misconceptions, stereotypes, and displays of ignorance have grown and developed out of colonialism, and these misunderstandings enable the strained relationship to continue between these two groups. This issue has been around for decades. Skinner points out, "Like Booker T. Washington, Du Bois was also exposed to the negative images of Africa held by almost all contemporary whites and most blacks in America."[9]

This all changed for me after my incidence of racial profiling, which helped me begin thinking of instances to help put me in the shoes of my American brothers and sisters. But before then, I had come in contact with a biracial friend whose name originated from Nigeria. I was first drawn to her as my countrywoman, then as an American. So, in putting down my sword, I was able to identify with my black brothers and sisters not only because of name affinity but by a common understanding of blackness. I then began focusing especially on how the conflict and tension potentially benefits other racial categories. This highlights the fact that conflict and

---

7. Konadu-Agyemang and Takyi, "Overview of African Immigration to US and Canada," 2.

8. Walker, *African Roots/American Cultures*, 232

9. Skinner, *African Americans and US Policy Toward Africa*, 171.

Part I | The Three Conversions of Peter

tension between both groups—Africans in Diaspora and African Americans—result directly from dominant White racial framing, wherein powerless groups are unable to effectively challenge the forces that oppress them, and thus attack themselves or people like themselves. I had to put down the sword of a judgmental attitude that most Africans of African origin hold toward black America, a sword that believes Black Americans waste or miss opportunities. In putting this sword down, I was able to begin engaging with my community. Peacemaking cannot be done in a vacuum. As I think of Peter, who was standing his ground against the outsiders that were coming to disturb the peace, their time, and experience with Jesus, such revelation leads me to no longer see black Americans as being disengaged with what is happening and instead to begin seeing them as allies in the work of peace, justice, and reconciliation.

Paul understood Jesus' intention and helped clarify it by writing about our true battle as a inner spiritual battle. In Ephesians 6:10–17, Paul painstakingly takes the time to explain what the battle will look like:

> "Finally, be strong in the Lord and his mighty power. Put on the full armor of God, so that you can take your stand against the devil's schemes. For our struggle is not against flesh and blood, but against the rulers, against the authorities, against the powers of this dark world and the spiritual forces of evil in the heavenly realms. Therefore, put on the full armor of God, so that when the day of evil comes, you may be able to stand your ground, and after you have done everything, to stand. Stand firm then, with the belt of truth buckled around your waist, with the breastplate of righteousness in place, and with your feet fitted with the readiness that comes from the gospel of peace. In addition to all this, take up the shield of faith, with which you can extinguish all the flaming arrows of the evil one. Take the helmet of salvation and the sword of the Spirit, which is the word of God." (NIV)

Paul clearly shows that such a battle is not physical, and so physical swords are not needed but rather spiritual ones. So, those who misunderstand, like Peter, tend to take a physical sword in response or for self-defense. But, misunderstanding Jesus' intent, this leads to the promotion of self-defense.

To put down our sword is to launch deep into the spiritual realm where we can find peace and joy. In doing so, we may need to listen to what John the Baptist says in John 3:30, "He must become greater; I must become less." Jesus continued to re-echo the call to eschew violence when he implored his disciples—and us today—to welcome the stranger, take care of the homeless, visit those incarcerated, etc.[10] When we do these things, we are no longer able to hold onto the sword that perpetrates violence against the other. As Christians, we have complicated that act of putting away the sword by categorizing it in theological terms and theological thoughts. Though it is meant to be simple, when it comes to the matter of Christianity and peacemaking, we are now faced with these theological challenges:

- The first challenge is some Christians tend to think of Christ's peace as mainly a personal peace with God. That is, it is just about me and God and that is all that matters, which is often followed by a sense of personal inner peace from a personal relationship with Jesus.

- The second challenge is to think of peace merely as the absence of conflict or any form of warfare, such as when two warring parties sign a peace treaty or when communities in conflict arrive at an agreed-upon resolution with a public pronouncement. Dr. King, in his "Letter from a Birmingham Jail," challenging the segregation that was happening in the South, he said, "segregation is not only politically, economically and sociologically unsound, but it is also morally wrong and sinful"[11] We need to remember Jesus was the one who blessed the peacemakers and therefore we should better figure out what that means. Indeed, by healing the ear of the one who came to arrest him, Jesus, through his act of peacemaking, demonstrated to us what he meant by stopping the violence and putting down our swords.

10. Matthew 25
11. King, "Letter from Birmingham Jail," para. 16.

Part I | The Three Conversions of Peter

What would that look like for us as North American Christian? What does that look like if we are not holding onto the armor of class and race? Peter was born into a high-class family and now that didn't matter anymore. He gave the best sermon, with a wonderful altar call, but that still didn't matter anymore. He was now going to do this unclean thing, go to a gentile's house and eat with him. Huh! Knowing that would make him unclean forever.

QUESTIONS FOR REFLECTION

- What swords do you carry? Where did you pick them up? Who or what are you trying to protect with your sword? Who are you ready to take down with your sword?

- What does it mean to put down your sword? How does putting down your sword look for you?

- Does your community put down its sword? If so, share with the group how that looks with stories and what you see as the outcome.

3
To Come without Objection

Radical Hospitality Is Necessary for Multicultural Peacemaking

"You shall treat the stranger who sojourns with you as the native among you, and you shall love him as yourself, for you were strangers in the land of Egypt: I am the Lord your God."

    Leviticus 19:34

"People will forget what you said, forget what you did, but people will never forget how you made them feel."[1]

    Maya Angelou

---

1. Angelou, *Maya Angelou*, 121.

PART I | THE THREE CONVERSIONS OF PETER

HOSPITALITY AS A FORM OF PEACEMAKING

Peter and Cornelius's encounter tells us about how much hospitality can be an instrument for peace. Cornelius was rich Peter was poor; Cornelius was well-educated, Peter was a common laborer; Cornelius was a gentile, a citizen of the powerful ruling nation, Peter was a Jew and under the control of Rome. But the Lord gave these two distinct people a love for one another that serves to show how every barrier can be broken if we allow the spirit to work in us.

I once heard a story about a white pastor in another city who, just as he was beginning his ministry, experienced something genuinely disruptive to his preconceived beliefs. He had befriended two black students from his youth group. While playing a game of tag one day with these young people, the pastor playfully managed to get one of the boys into a headlock. In that moment, rather than relishing his victory, he immediately released the young man, throwing his hands into the air and shouting the young man's name. Thinking the pastor might be injured, the other young man ran to his aid. Realizing that he was not injured, the boys stood baffled. Looking at the boy, the pastor said quietly, "You have soft hair."

Immediately, the young man touched his hair and responded, "Yes, of course."

All three of them stared at each other for a few moments. Then the pastor said, "Do you know what I was told about black people? Do you know what I have always thought? I was told that all black people have hair like steel wool, but yours is soft."

At that moment, the pastor realized what he had been told his entire life about the hair of black people was wrong. This truth broke through learned falsehoods because he had taken the time to befriend people different from himself and allowed himself to enter their lives, even to the point of touching their hair. From that point on, the pastor had to reexamine whatever else he had been told about others, acknowledging it might not be true.

In order to grapple with our reality, people often have to be faced with truth in order to reorient their way of thinking. Reorientation requires the management of our memories. We easily get stuck on things that have happened to us or to people we have known, holding onto past wounds and history. We see this pattern very clearly when the memories or beliefs are racially or religiously inclined. To move beyond this sort of reaction, as that pastor was able to do, we must do the hard work of managing and reconsidering feelings and assumptions, so that we can be open to a new way of relating with one another. We must unlearn our biases and embedded beliefs by experiencing reality and allowing it to formulate new truths.

OUR APPROACH TO HOSPITALITY: POLITE

When it comes to hospitality, many in our culture readily equate hospitality with a generic friendliness. In a way it is like being a therapeutic nice guy who asks only that we be nice too: the result misses the essence of true hospitality. We do less hospitality and more entertaining. In entertaining, we expect someone to show up to our house for a full meal, eat at a scheduled time, and then leave at a scheduled time, with conversations often framed around, "Oh, that couch is beautiful," or "Is that a new couch?" or "Oh, don't look at my house, it is such a mess," all while zigzagging from that to, "Did I show you the new addition we made upstairs?"

This kind of hospitality has become so much about sharing about our stuff, our home improvement projects, our planned vacation, our pets, etc. Our culture has developed a ritual of gift-giving, such as bringing a flower or a bottle of wine to the hostess, etc. I don't in any way fault these, but in such sharings we tend to miss the radical practice of graciously welcoming one another, especially the stranger, as God has welcomed us.

Can genuine hospitality, which once was central to Christians' way of doing life together, be recovered? The form of hospitality that Scripture calls us to practice, like loving your neighbor and even loving your enemy and doing good to those who persecute you. Today we have relegated some of these great ancient practices to the likes of Starbucks and restaurants, who are now responsible for creating a welcome space for us to be entertained.

Part I | The Three Conversions of Peter

Recovering this ancient tradition is essential in a world that has grown divisive and harsh. These ancient practices have the potential of turning enemy into friends. Doing that will take some intentionality as expressed in the story of Peter and Cornelius. Both were once on different sides of a divide—Cornelius a Roman Military officer, Peter a follower of Jesus, who was subservient to the Roman military occupiers.

The practice of hospitality in the church means to participate in God's peaceable kingdom, as Darrell Guder, observed: "Such hospitality indicates the crossing of boundaries (ethnic origin, economic condition, political orientation, gender status, social experience, educational background) by being open and welcoming of the other. Without such communities of hospitality, the world will have no way of knowing that all God's creation is meant to live in peace"[2].

UNTAMED HOSPITALITY

While our culture reduces hospitality to friendliness that provides private entertainment, Christian hospitality reminds us it extends beyond entertainment. How do we shift gears to practice this untamed hospitality? The practice of untamed hospitality goes beyond just an invitation for coffee to the form of hospitality, where the guest being received is offered a drink, but one which is beyond water. While our culture reduces hospitality to friendliness that provides private entertainment, Christian hospitality extends beyond entertainment. How do we shift gears to practice this untamed hospitality? A hospitality form that goes beyond just an invitation for coffee to which the guest feels genuinely welcomed beyond just a drink. Genuine hospitality is always more than helping a friend or providing for the stranger, and it is an attitude of the heart "that moves over to allow true space for the other"[3]. However, the offering of a drink of water is the simplest way to pledge friendship with a person. When Eliezer, Abraham's servant, sought a welcome, he

---

2. Conner, "Darrell L. Guder," 5.
3. Kathy Callahan-Howell in Finding Home (p. 67).

did so by requesting of the maiden who came to the well to draw water "Let me, I pray thee, drink a little water from thy pitcher." And when she answers, "Drink, my lord." Genesis 24:17, 18. At that point Eliezer knew he was welcomed.

That act was an indication he was welcome to be a guest at the nearby home. With this significance attached to a drink of water, the following promise of Jesus takes on new meaning: "Whosoever shall give you a cup of water to drink in my name, because ye belong to Christ, verily I say unto you, he shall not lose his reward" (Mark 9:4). The guest served a meal. The sharing of food in the ancient Near East is a very special act of hospitality. It means far more than it means in our fast-service culture. It is a way of making a covenant of peace and fidelity. When Abimelech wanted a permanent covenant with Isaac, the confirmation of that covenant came when Isaac "made them a feast, and they did eat and drink" (Gen 26:26).

One hallmark of the early Christian community, from its inception to the Pastoral Epistles authored by Paul, was the call for those who show hospitality to be elected to the office of leadership in the faith community: "Now the overseer is to be above reproach, faithful to his wife, temperate, self-controlled, respectable, hospitable, able to teach" (1 Tim 3:2). For the first two centuries of the early church, followers of Jesus met in homes. Hospitality became an important and necessary element in the life of the church. As Christianity began to spread, moving out of homes into buildings, there was a shift in the meaning of hospitality. Not only would the church provide hospitality to one another as followers of Christ, it became a place where people under attack could find refuge or sanctuary. The safety of the building could not be violated by the state. The church's understanding of hospitality began to shift to resemble the offering of a place of safety and refuge in a sacrificial manner.

SACRIFICIAL HOSPITALITY

Abraham, the man called "righteous" because of his faith (Jas 2:23), was a great example of hospitality that we can follow. The

Part I | The Three Conversions of Peter

story of Abraham's hospitality is often the focus of the scene in the story in Genesis 18:1–16. Abraham had encounters with the angel of the Lord, who made a promise to him that Sarah was going to bear a son. While that is a beneficial teaching from this passage, something else is illustrated as well, which is Abraham's willingness and eagerness of heart to extend hospitality to these three men who, unbeknownst to him, turned out to be angels.

Abraham's hospitality was on display when he rushed to Sarah and asked her to get out the fine flour and make enough fine bread to feed what we would today call august visitors. He also took the fattened calf and made a meal that seemed to be for a special occasion and not merely for strange travelers that were simply passing by.

We only find out later in the Scripture reading that these men were in fact angels and one might even be Christ himself (Gen 18:1, 10) as the use of the term LORD (which is the highly personal name of God or Yahweh) these verses suggests. This kind of hospitality is a radical display of what it would actually means to build a mountain that is above other mountains.

Another prominent story of hospitality that is worth noting appears in 1 Kings 17, where the prophet Elijah bursts onto the scene and confronts King Ahab with a pronouncement about the weather. Elijah's story brings many questions to mind. Who is this guy and where does he come from? I would in no way attempt to answer these questions but would rather focus on God's act of hospitality through these stories.

Not so much by way of background is told about Elijah except that he is "from Tishbe in Gilead." There had been seven kings since the separation between the Northern and Southern Kingdoms. This story took place in the Northern Kingdom of Israel. Many of the kings had been evil, continuing the sins of idolatry that their fathers had committed, and I beg to say they had lost the act of hospitality as outlined in the Deuteronomistic passages. In 1 Kings 15:26, when Ahab came onto the scene, everything at this point had sunk to an all-time low. Ahab had married Jezebel—a foreigner—and Ahab allowed Jezebel to introduce to the people the worship of other gods such as Baal.

Baal worship of course was a form of idolatry. Baal was the god of the weather, purported to have the power over rainfall and the different seasons, and supposedly had the power to appoint the time of each season. Furthermore, Baal served as the god of nature and fertility, and because much of the people's livelihood depended on rain, they forgot what it meant to depend on the God of Israel who delivered them from bondage and took them to the promised land.

It was against this backdrop that the prophet Elijah told Ahab there wouldn't be any more rain until he (Elijah) said so. Elijah's statement undoubtedly prepared the grounds for a direct confrontation between God and Baal. What then happened, 1 Kings 17:2–3 tells us, "Then the LORD said to Elijah, go to the east and hide by Kerith Brook. . ." Elijah then went off to hide as God had promised to provide for his needs. First, God accomplished that using the ravens; soon enough, the brook ran dry. Note that Elijah had called for rain to stop and that meant there was no rain in the land.

Drought was in progress. Elijah was then instructed to go to Zarephath to be cared for by a widow: "Then the LORD said to Elijah, 'Go and live in the village of Zarephath, near the city of Sidon. There is a widow there who will feed you. I have given her my instructions'" (1 Kgs 17:8–9). Elijah requested of the widow a "bite of bread" (1 Kgs 17:12). Pushed to the brink of losing her livelihood and her hospitality, the widow responded in honesty and told Elijah of her situation. Elijah, however, urged her not to be afraid: "Go ahead and cook that 'last meal,' but bake me a little loaf of bread first. Afterward there will still be enough food for you and your son. For this is what the LORD, the God of Israel, says: "There will always be plenty of flour and oil left in your containers until the time when the LORD sends rain and the crops grow again""" (1 Kgs 17:13–14). This widow's act of hospitality showed her obedience to Elijah's directives. And because of this, she was blessed with the miraculous provision of daily supplies: "For no matter how much they used, there was always enough left in the containers, just as the LORD had promised through Elijah" (1 Kgs 17:16).

Hospitality from a biblical perspective is to recognize that God is more interested in caring relationships than the process by which they are expressed. No matter if we live in a single-room apartment or a split-level ranch, the only real requirement is allowing God to use our lives and our willingness. Hospitality is not about showing off your house, your decorating skills, or your cooking abilities; it is not just having friends over to play games, although that can be an element of it; it is not about you or your possessions. Hospitality is about God and how he uses you and your possessions to serve those who come into contact with you, be they friends or strangers, believers or unbelievers. Hospitality is about investing in others' lives and learning how you can best serve those around you. We can think of this act of hospitality in terms of our own experience in helping people to come to and experience God.

RADICAL EXPRESSION OF HOSPITALITY

In recent years, the USA has witnessed an influx of refugees fleeing violence and conflict in their countries and seeking a safe place. A few churches have offered their sanctuaries as places of refuge for these immigrants. These churches and even some cities have begun restoring the image of the church as a sanctuary, offering hospitality to those fleeing conflict and arrest by Immigration and Custom Enforcement (ICE).

One particular modern-day example of hospitality which puts Christianity against government intervention is the story of a 53-year-old, undocumented immigrant from Mexico who was facing deportation after thirty years of living in the United States.[4] This woman's decision to take refuge in a church re-echoes the Christian call to hospitality. In her story, as reported by different news outlets, she, like thousands of other refugees, had to flee dehumanizing conditions back home. It was similar to the early Christians under Roman occupation who ran away from threats to their lives following violent atrocities perpetrated by the Roman authorities.

Another instance of hospitality as an element of peacemaking can be seen through this act of kindness by a church in Columbus,

---

4. McCrummen, "Sanctuary of One."

Ohio. In October 2017, a Columbus church took in an immigrant who was seeking shelter. Edith Espinal, along with her two daughters, was fleeing abuse from her home country. At the time of their taking refuge in this church, they had been living in the US for over twenty years as asylum seekers. Suddenly, ICE came up with a draconian act of deporting immigrants in the US, including asylum seekers. This church swung into action to protect asylum seekers like Edith and her children. This mostly white congregation of about 200 people gave sanctuary to over fifty immigrants in their church. This and several other churches across the country, as reported by the Church World Service, have become de facto sanctuaries because immigration authorities generally avoid enforcing deportation orders by entering "sensitive" locations, including churches, hospitals, courthouses, and schools.[5]

In an ever-changing time, when cities like Chicago, New York, Los Angeles, and more are taking the title of "sanctuary city" and offering refuge, the church's calling remains to offer the best hospitality. Despite changes within American church culture, Christian hospitality remains one of the hallmarks of the church. In neglecting to show hospitality to immigrants and refugees, many of whom are fleeing all manner of violence and threat, the church is degrading and rejecting one of its ultimate calls from Scripture.

For most early Christians, an absence of hospitality would mean an absence of love for God and neighbor. This perspective can be seen vividly in Luke's writings. Let's explore some of Luke's emphasis on hospitality in three passages that are unique to his work: Luke 10:1–16, Luke 24:13–35, and Acts 9:43—10:48. In 10:1–16, Luke describes Jesus' commissioning of the seventy disciples who will travel in pairs to various towns to spread the news about the message of the kingdom. Jesus instructs the seventy to depend on the hospitality of the townspeople they encounter. For instance, he prohibits them from carrying their own provisions. Instead, the blessing and peace of God will rest upon those hosts who extend hospitality to Jesus' servants.

---

5. Karas, "Tale of Two Sanctuary Churches."

Part I | The Three Conversions of Peter

Permit me to stress, once more, a wider sense of care for those affected by violence, not only for refugees from other countries, but also to inner-city youth facing violence. The youth population in many cities across America are faced with an unprecedented scourge of violence, as well as daily pressure to join gangs or else face the wrath of gang leaders.

Faith communities have chosen to uphold the Christian heritage of hospitality, seeking to show the world their actions can restore peace and transform conflict. As people of faith, our actions must move toward portraying a scripturally based, nonviolent resistance to the violence that is being perpetrated on our young people. Although people may carry old stereotypes of cynicism and suspicion, the hope is these positive actions will be warmly welcomed within the communities where violence is most overt and prevalent.

The early Christian practice of hospitality is one viable model for peacebuilding that is backed by a nonviolent approach to solving this problem. Until recently, a group of Christians in my community took actions through a radical expression of hospitality to a community ravaged by gang activities. Such acts of hospitality led to a reduction in gang-related violence. In this case, they saw the need to show hospitality toward the other, not just to those they felt connected to but also to those who felt they were outsiders in their midst.

QUESTIONS FOR REFLECTION

- Should your local church offer sanctuary to anyone who seeks it? Have you offered sanctuary? Describe it.

- The early practice of Christian hospitality led to exponential growth in the church. How does hospitality look in your home and your church?

- Does your local church offer sanctuary to undocumented immigrants? If so, how did you make the decision? If you don't, why not? If someone asked for sanctuary, would you grant it?

PART II

To Be Conscious of Our Sin
The Commandments and Pathways of Peace

Therefore no one will be declared righteous in God's sight by the works of the law; rather, through the law we become conscious of our sin.

ROMANS 3:20 (NIV)

CHAPTER 4: EYE FOR AN EYE, TOOTH FOR A TOOTH: OLD TESTAMENT LAW IN A NEW TESTAMENT WORLD

Objective: The violence of our community is not incident based.

When Rev. Dr. Martin Luther King Jr preached about the triple violence of capitalism, racism and militarism he was speaking of a violence that was oppressive at all levels, so built into the hierarchies and systems of our cultures that it was nearly invisible. The violence's he described are still with us, so interwoven with us as individual, in our communities, and enshrined in the laws of our government that they seem impossible to root out. Yet, I have witnessed how people of faith and committed to peacemaking can bring an awareness and begin the process of building justice and peace. Moving to South Africa, a few years of the dismantling of Apartheid I witnessed how the Truth and Reconciliation process offered many people a spiritual path forward. In Rockford, Illinois, it took a shooting for us to begin to build bridges between the East and West sides off town, across decades of segregation and classism.

CHAPTER 5: RAIN FALLS ON THE JUST AND THE UNJUST: A VISION FOR PEACE AFTER THE COVID-19 PLAGUE

Objective: How to be a peacemaker when "bad things" are happening to all of us

Covid-19 and racial violence, being acknowledged with a new awareness around the world, are being called a double pandemic. It has felt impossible to address either when one is not a virologist and unable to gather as a community in traditional peacemaking models. It is a time when all of us feel at risk—and all of us feel culpable. Just as we might be unknowingly carrying the novel coronavirus, we are possibly hurting others by being part of the racist hierarchies in our daily lives. Yet, it has always been this way. We have to be able to offer a community response that breaks the cycle even though it might not be the thing that save us. This making tool, making peace with our own vulnerability and guilt, has enabled Rockford to address the long-term impacts of racial profiling and school to prison pipelines by interrupting the education inequalities.

CHAPTER 6: TABLES IN THE TEMPLE: IS THERE SUCH A THING AS RIGHTEOUS VIOLENCE

Objective: Acknowledge why this feels right and remember why we cannot "go there"

But Jesus overturned the tables in the temples…it is too easy to read that Scripture as a way to justify violence as Christians. However, we must acknowledge that Jesus also healed the blind and made the lame walk—things we cannot do. When we begin to do violence as Christians, in the name of religion, we begin to be part of the legacy of empirical power using faith to dominate others that goes back to colonialism, antebellum slavery, and genocide of indigenous peoples in the names of "gold, glory and God."

4

Eye for an Eye, Tooth for a Tooth

Old Testament Law in a New Testament World

"You have heard that it was said, 'Eye for eye, and tooth for tooth. 39 But I tell you, do not resist an evil person. If anyone slaps you on the right cheek, turn to them the other cheek also"

MATTHEW 5:38-39

"One of the most difficult things is not to change society but to change yourself."[1]

NELSON MANDELA

Jesus and his disciples were once again in this foreign land, the land of Samaria. It was once recognized as the birthplace of the Jewish faith. Genesis 12 gives us an account of Abraham's encounter with God in Samaria and Shechem. In that encounter, God promised Abraham that "this land would belong to [his] descendants" (Gen 17:8). History tells us when the Israelites were defeated by

---

1. Ricard, *Altruism*, 15.

the Assyrians, they settled in the land, making it a settlement for a mostly mixed population. So, when Jesus arrived on the scene of history, the people of Israel viewed the Samaritans with a bit of mixed feelings. Yet, we see Jesus' trip into this territory was to break the walls of hostility that existed.

On this day, Jesus encountered a woman of Samaria at a well. She had come out during the day to fetch water for her household. Jesus proceeded to ask her for a drink, to which this woman responded, "What? A Jew asking a Samarian for water? Where have you been? Because Jews don't drink after Samaritans, not to talk of asking for a drink." Jesus, in his classic response, said, "If you only know who was asking you for a drink, you would ask him for a living water. Because everyone who drinks of the water out of this well will be thirsty again, but those who drink that water I give will never thirst again" (John 4:14). A lot of things come to mind from this encounter. There is a male and female encounter, and there is the racial separation between Jews and Samaritans.

What we have heard Jesus talk about in the Sermon on the Mount is not so much an outright moral obligation but an opportunity for the world to see an expression of what the kingdom of God could look like. Jesus' teaching compels us not to repay evil with evil but be kind, even as expressed in Jesus, a Jew, asking for a drink from a Samaritan, which goes against tradition but serves to demonstrate a breaking of manmade racial, cultural, socioeconomic, language-based, and social-class barriers. This is precisely why the Sermon on the Mount is so challenging and disorienting. When taken seriously, as followers of Jesus we are called to live in the company of Jesus, always with access to the kingdom of heaven. It is not the way the world operates; it is a description of another world that is planted within this world until that kingdom fully comes to fruition. As followers of Jesus, we are like people from another planet in our radical obedience to the teachings of Jesus; if not, then we have missed our calling.

As I said earlier, if Jesus had only stated these things without actually demonstrating what they meant, he may not have had the followers he had. Worse still, these followers would not have stuck with him that long. That is why when he said to his disciples "follow me," they left everything: their fishing boats, their tax booth, their treasury business, etc., to follow him. They saw something in him which compelled them to take up his offer. "The greatest thing a human soul ever does in this world is to see something and tell what it saw in a plain way. Hundreds of people can talk for one who can think, but thousands can think for one who can see. To see clearly is poetry, prophecy and religion, all in one."[2]

Jesus taught the content of the kingdom, he created the space for which it made sense to his listeners. Before he gave the answer, he elicited the right question and curiosity. He first won the allegiances of listeners of followers, demonstrating to them what the love of God is. And if this is what the love of God looks like in action, where there are no outsiders and everyone is an insider first, this attracts people from every point on the compass.

What Jesus says is totally antithetical to the typical attitude you find these days. Years ago, there was a bumper sticker that became very popular with two simple words: "I want." Now that statement can be attached to just about everything under the sun, as it were. We live in a time of "I want." I want my rights; I want my happiness; I want my way; I want my comfort; I want my revenge—all these are counter to the call to sacrifice and to let go by letting God.

SOUTH AFRICA: RACE, APARTHEID, AND SPIRITUALITY

Apartheid can simply be described as a word that means "separation" and "separate development of people based on skin color and ethnic origins." The roots of apartheid can be traced to nineteenth-century colonial development. By the "early 20th century, British colonial administrators decided to adopt a policy of separate development based on the teachings of John Ruskin."[3] Ruskin was an art critic of the Victorian era, whose writings emphasized the connections between nature, art, and society. His teachings claimed that in an

---

2. Ruskin, John, and Charles Eliot Norton. *The Correspondence of John Ruskin and Charles Eliot Norton*. Cambridge University Press, 1987.66

3. Ross et al., *Cambridge History of South Africa*, 2:143.

ideal society, the superior white race would assist the other races to work toward the eventual goal of equality and reintegration, all while maintaining a degree of separation between them. These "lesser" races would be given tasks more suited to their mental and physical progression.[4]

In the 1920s, laws were passed to facilitate the legal separation of people by their physical attributes associated with skin color and hair texture. Laws passed in South Africa were similar to the ones passed in the United States in the aftermath of reconstruction. For instance, Black South Africans would no longer be allowed to enter White urban areas. These practices rendered everyone a prisoner in the country to which they belonged. People of European descent had more rights and enjoyed greater luxury, while Black Africans, Indians, and Indigenous people of southern Africa (*Koisans*) were relegated to manual labor for their white counterparts (oppressors).

Many White and Black South Africans of all creeds did not turn a blind eye to the unfairness brought about by this policy, and protests all across the country, as well as from many countries around the world grew steadily. Eventually, economic sanctions and diplomatic pressure forced change. President F. W. de Klerk "responded to the pressure by allowing several political parties to become legal again, culminating in the release of Nelson Mandela from prison."[5] Mandela had been imprisoned by the South African government because his appeal to majority Black and marginalized communities was seen as threat to the government, which could have led to an uprising, violence by the citizens, and a loss of position and wealth for Whites.

Mandela's release from prison led to the first truly "free and fair elections in the country. These elections resulted in the African National Congress (ANC) being voted into power and Nelson Mandela taking the seat as president,"[6] rising from prisoner of the system to leading the system. Amazingly, this transition of power occurred peacefully. "The injustices of apartheid were explained

---

4. Ross et al., *Cambridge History of South Africa*, 145.
5. Bouckaert, "Negotiated Revolution," 375.
6. Bouckaert, "Negotiated Revolution," 280.

away as an experiment that did not work. Although apartheid may no longer be the national policy in South Africa, the system certainly took its toll on the country."[7] There are many long-lasting consequences following the elevation of one race at the expense of others.

While many citizens have moved forward, embracing every "ethnic nationality and race as fellow South Africans,"[8] some white people still hold on to the old mindset of being racially superior. Perhaps these very circumstances have made South Africa, "one of the world's leaders in dealing with racial issues and political inequities. Whatever the case, the country has become and continues to be unified,"[9] by its many colorful people who continue to work toward racial and socioeconomic integration instead of being torn apart by its differences.

In South Africa, the Truth and Reconciliation Commission, which was formed at the end of apartheid, became the bedrock for transition from repressive rule to a democracy. The Truth and Reconciliation commission was to be a crucial component of South Africa's transition to being a full and free democratic country, while promoting national unity and reconciliation in a spirit of understanding which transcends the conflicts and divisions of the past.

USA: SYSTEMIC RACISM AND CLASSISM (ROCKFORD EAST AND WEST SIDE DIVIDE)

Growing up in Nigeria, I heard much about the American Dream. It captured the imagination of many of my peers and centered around the myth that if you work hard you will make it out of poverty. It also put forth the idea that America is a colorblind society. But when I moved to America, I realized what I had been told was not the whole truth: racism exists every bit as much as the possibility of attaining the American Dream. Americans would "like to think of

---

7. Bouckaert, "Negotiated Revolution," 295.
8. Bouckaert, "Negotiated Revolution," 296.
9. Seekings and Nattrass, *Class, Race, and Inequality in South Africa*, 49.

the founding of the American colonies, and later, the United States, as driven by a quest for freedom, religious liberty, and political and economic independence."[10] However, racial inequality has shaped American history since the arrival of White people in the land. "From the start, American society was founded with systems of domination, inequality, and oppression particularly the denial of freedom for African slaves. One of the great paradoxes of American history is the coexistence of the ideals of equality and freedom with practice of slavery."[11] Today "we live with the ramifications of that paradox,"[12] most clearly seen in our inner cities, where racial divides are drawn and many of the youth feel disconnected.

Nowadays when people ask me where I am from, I say Rockford, Illinois. I am not trying to deny Jos, Nigeria or Cape Town, South Africa—I am also from these places—it is simply because Rockford has become a part of me, a place where I feel welcomed, and a place I understand. In my time here, I have seen the impact of centuries of racial division in this community. This history and my contemporary experience continue to shape my ministry and call to better understand how racial oppression imposes harm on people. Nevertheless, "to think of racism as something that only affects the lives of African Americans, Native Americans, Asian Americans, Latinos and other racially defined minorities is a mistake."[13] American society has been profoundly shaped by race and politics, both of which have equally affected white and blacks in deeply negative ways, but on a general level its negative impact on white people can appear to be less than for other minorities. These perceptions have led to an increase in violent conflict.

GETTING THE BALL ROLLING

My experiences of growing up in Nigeria in a predominantly Muslim community, my friendship with Haruna, and my travel and

10. Huntington, *Who Are We?*, 40
11. Huntington, *Who Are We?*, 23.
12. Huntington, *Who Are We?*, 24.
13. Hollinger, *Postethnic America*, 4.

work in South Africa and now living in Rockford, Illinois, as well as my studies in the academic field of conflict transformation and Kingian nonviolence, have given me a unique skill set. This serves as a foundational base to lead these groups, helping them to envision what change could look like for the Center for Nonviolence and Conflict Transformation (CNCT) as an organization, and for the community of Rockford.

And as a church planter, who's theologically grounded in peace and reconciliation, also seizing on experiences, I used that as a basis to share with the group the transformation process that would have to happen. My goal was to help develop a replicable model of peacemaking in North American cities, suburbs, and around the world, grounded in Anabaptist beliefs. It was not enough to document my personal experience alone; I also needed to demonstrate other participants' diversity in this organization. I see myself as a facilitator working toward the goal of the Abrahamic faiths working together.

Because it is crucial to have basic principles undergirding our working together, I developed simple ground rules for us to begin. This process must start with the recognition that Abraham is the patriarch of not just Christianity, but Islam and Judaism as well. Each of these faiths claim Abraham as their father. They theologically agree that God is sovereign and the Creator of the universe. In this process of working together, agreement that there should be no proselytization of one another is imperative.

As we began working together, I came into contact with the Kingian nonviolence approach to leadership development and in turn introduced these methods of leadership development to the group. The Kingian nonviolence approach is comprised of the simple principles that were developed from Dr. Martin Luther King's work and writings, most especially from his book, *Stride Toward Freedom*.[14] These principles helped to galvanize leadership development during the civil rights movement of the fifties and sixties:

1. Nonviolence is a way of life for courageous people. Simply put, nonviolence is a positive force that confronts injustice by

---

14. King, Jr., *Stride Toward Freedom*, 35.

utilizing the righteous anger, the spiritual, the emotional, and the intellectual capability to bring change and transformation.
2. The beloved community is the framework for the future. To achieve meaningful reconciliation and transformation, raising relationships to the level where justice prevails and everyone has the ability to attain their full human potential is required.
3. Attack the forces of evil, not persons doing evil. In this approach, identify the underlying harmful conditions, such as policies and practices, rather than reacting to people and personalities.
4. Accept suffering without retaliation for the sake of the cause to achieve the goal. In this principle, self-chosen suffering is seen as redemptive in helping one grow spiritually and also in one's human dimension. Here, the moral authority of voluntary suffering is a goal for addressing the community's concerns.
5. Avoid internal violence of the spirit as well as external physical violence. This provision is of a mirror reflection on the reality of the condition of one's opponent and the community at large.
6. "The universe is on the side of justice."[15] Because truth is universal in all of human society, humans are created and endowed with a sense of justice and doing right. These three religions attest to the sense of justice and peace.[16] [/NL 1–6]

Coupled with the aforementioned ground rules, these principles provided a model for how we would operate together to address the violent conflict witnessed in our community. These principles need to be developed within us individually and collectively in order to see the systemic change we hope for occur, with the expectation that relationships even between conflicting parties will be improved. Kingian nonviolence theory proposes that when a diverse group of people spends extended time studying these principles together, the study will enable them to have a common framework from which to work. This framework has the potential to transform their conflict, causing any negative stereotypes they have of each other to gradually decrease and possibly even disappear.

15. LaFayette and Jehnsen, *Leader's Manual*, 44.
16. LaFayette and Jehnsen, *Leader's Manual*, 45.

Unlike our work in past group experiences and other contexts, these Kingian nonviolence leadership development principles became a guiding philosophy, and with practical application in our work they bound us together as a group. It is now my practice to use these six principles as a curriculum for training any new member who seeks to join the group, as well as to incorporate them into ongoing monthly refreshers for the existing group. As with any diverse group, not all participants have the same set of social skills, causing me to wonder how I might motivate people to interact or socialize with one another across faith traditions.

To remove every barrier that could hinder socialization and group interaction, I invited Dr. David Jensen, a respected civil rights leader from the sixties, to Rockford. Jenson was one of Dr. King's protégés and remains a living witness, able to share his experiences of working with different religions and denominations during the Civil Rights movement.

In his presentation, Dr. Jensen shared how different religious groups working together helped to galvanize the success of the Civil Rights movement. He also explained how the six principles were developed as a working guideline for leadership development for those willing to participate in the act of civil disobedience during protest marches.

I continue to teach the different faith leaders, as well as others who aspire to become leaders, what it means to be a conflict transformer. The teachings shift from emphasizing interpersonal conflict transformation to accepting the responsibility to become a part of transforming the community on religious, racial, ethnic, socioeconomic, class, and gender diversity levels.

The chief goal for training leaders is to equip them for action when acts of violence are committed. Doing this has helped me identify what I call landmarks as signs of transformation which will produce a lasting change personally and communally. The model I developed is unique in that it goes beyond the historical practice of mediation, restorative justice practice, and conflict reconciliation. These latter strategies have not been very effective in transforming violent conflict. Education and training alone cannot do it either;

but an ongoing, nonviolent conflict transformation process is beginning to produce the needed systemic change.

The act of bringing the Abrahamic faiths together to work from their different theological peace positions, while adding a layer of Dr. King's philosophy of nonviolence conflict reconciliation, has helped build a community of reconciled people. CNCT's application of the Kingian nonviolence theory into our community's praxis has included the development of our mobile tech lab and mobile art lab, and combining racial and socioeconomic realities with restoring relationships between police and the community.

TRIPLE VIOLENCE AS DESCRIBED BY MLK (CAPITALISM, RACISM, AND MILITARISM)

Capitalism revolves around the private ownership of the means of production, market allocation, and corporate divisions of labor. It remunerates property, power, and to a limited extent contribution to output. Class divisions arise from differences in property ownership and access to empowered work versus subservient work. Class divisions create huge differences in decision-making influence and quality of life."[17]

American mythology asserts that capitalism and democracy go hand in hand, but in reality, capitalism slowly eats away at our freedom. Samuel Bowles and Herbert Gintis have pointed out that, "a market arena of self-interested and anonymous interaction might reduce not only the need for compassion, but also the sentiment itself. In this respect, the economy produces people as well as things, and the capitalist economy produces people that are not ideally equipped with the democratic sentiments and capacities."[18]

Not only does capitalism make us less civil, it also helps organize us in a way that limits our choices. Capitalism, at its best, seeks to build a boundary between the public and private spheres in a way that constrains the comprehension of true individual freedom, reducing the scope of what it means to be free

---

17. Baddon, et al., *People's Capitalism?*, 54.
18. Finn, *Moral Ecology of Markets*, 21.

and democratic. The result is a few elites controlling the political system, governments serving the interests of private capitalists, and very limited freedom for workers. So, does all that mean I prefer socialism? Or anarchism? Or libertarianism? Heck no. The Jesus socioeconomic system describes how much easier it is for a camel to go through the eye of a needle than for a rich man to enter the kingdom of God (Matt 19:24).

For any "nation that continues year after year to spend more money on military defense than on programs of social uplift is approaching spiritual death."[19] In the same speech, King makes the point of emphasizing the three evils of society, extending a call for anyone who wants to be engaged with the global condition to be aware of what is ravaging and affecting humans today, such as militarism, racism, and capitalism.

This age of "an eye for an eye" and "a tooth for a tooth," when fused with racism, militarism, and materialism, is a perfect recipe for total destruction. This has wreaked havoc on the destiny of the entire world. It has undermined previous agreements on the international stage, such as the Geneva Agreement, the Climate Agreement, and others. It has also impaired the work of the United Nations, an umbrella organization we all have come to rely on for international guidance on global issues.

So, to address this problem, MLK called for "a radical revolution of values,"[20] a revolution that demands people adjust their priorities in order to address injustice. But such a revolution must be value-centered, moving away from taking the safe road and not challenging the status quo. Now is the time to ask: Is the current challenge ravaging the world worth ignoring?

Although I find it somewhat difficult to preach the prophetic words of Scripture, I am inspired by the words of Amos, Isaiah, Jeremiah, Ezekiel, and the greatest prophet of all: Jesus. These words call for a personal commitment to change; they make us feel guilty, and because they demand a social change, they make us feel angry and overwhelmed. Yes, the words about justice in the Scriptures are

---

19. King, "America's Chief Moral Dilemma," 36:15–36:29.
20. King, *Radical King*, 11:15.

disturbing. If I talk about them, some won't like them. If I preach about them, maybe some will respond positively while others will respond in the negative. The fact is, the word "justice" feels alien to the church. It is a word that appears eighty-three times in the Old Testament and thirty-four times in the New Testament. The word simply means "rightness." The way we move toward the kingdom of God is to move toward justice. Justice is simply the reality that God is with us.

I could go on and on, pulling stories from the Scriptures that talk about the love of God, the forgiveness of God, and the compassion of God, which has far-reaching implications for our world. These stories talk about righteousness with God and righteousness amongst the people of God, stories which talk to us about God's justice, eliminating "an eye for an eye" justice and replacing it with the kingdom.

Now that you have the overview, I invite you to join me on this pathway to peace. I guarantee there will be some personal as well as systemic transformation as a result of this life-changing process.

QUESTIONS FOR REFLECTION

Let's begin with the recognition that our ethnic and religious identities are important to God. Without them, we have a limited understanding of who God is. Ask one or two people from another Abrahamic faith to share their story with you. Listen to their stories and their views of God's desire for peace and conflict transformation. If you don't know someone from one of the Abrahamic faiths, read about that faith from a reputable source—not what others say about them, but what they say about their beliefs and practices of peace and conflict transformation. See if you can find some areas of connection between your religious beliefs. Also, search for some areas of human connection between your faith and theirs, and write them down.

- Do you have suggestions for ways to improve a working relationship?

- What does courage mean to you?
- When you think of the beloved community, whom are you referring to?
- Would you be willing to host a community conversation?

5

Rain Falls on the Just and the Unjust

A Vision for Peace After the Covid-19 Plague

"He has shown you, O mortal, what is good and what does the Lord require of you? To act justly and to love mercy and toe walk humbly with your God"

    Micah 6:8

"Justice is love correcting that which revolts against love."[1]

    MLK, January 30th 1959

BESIEGED BY COVID-19

There's the old saying that the rain falls on the just and the unjust alike, but looking at the impact of Covid-19, one cannot say this because minority communities in many cities across America are being disproportionately besieged by a virus that acts like an

---

1. Gabel, "Spiritual Dimension of Social Justice," 673.

Rain Falls on the Just and the Unjust

invading army. However, we have not been besieged by an army but by a plague. Covid-19 spreads primarily through droplets of saliva or discharges from the nose when an infected person coughs or sneezes. It has become important for people to practice respiratory etiquette since, at the time of this writing, there are no specific vaccines or treatments for Covid-19. This virus infects the just and the unjust, invading people's lives and livelihood.

In AD 165, a mysterious plague killed millions of Europeans. This plague reshaped the centuries that followed for Europeans in the medieval era. It was such a big deal that they named it Antonine Plague, and, just as Covid-19 is reshaping our lives, it will continue to reshape the twenty-first century.

In AD 165, Rome was the most flourishing empire on earth. There were two ruling classes: philosopher and warrior. Marcus Aurelius was the ruler of the warrior class. This ruling class had just returned from West Asia, where they had conquered the lands and the people, and brought back their spoils of war. But, unbeknown to Marcus, one of the spoils he and his army brought back was a disease which had severely impacted East Asia. As the army marched back to Rome, the disease began to manifest, and it soon spread everywhere they went, first in Asia Minor, then Greece.

The mysterious epidemic spread like wildfire, particularly through the densely populated Roman cities of Italy. The Romans controlled the entire Mediterranean, and as their trading ships and armies busily swarmed across it, so did the disease. At the height of that epidemic, there were fatalities of up to about 2,000 people dying per day, according to Roman sources.[2] In total, it was estimated that about 7–10 percent of the Roman Empire was killed. The plague swept over Spain, Italy, Greece, Asia Minor, and even into Egypt.

Although we are separated from Ancient Rome by nearly 2000 years, the description of how cities reacted to this pandemic seems to be alike, as we today acknowledge that the numbers of the dead have been beyond anything that anyone could have imagined at the outset. It is also worth noting that the famous classical physician

2. Ibid, 83.

Galan lived through the plague and reported on the manner in which the inhabitants of Rome were dying, writing that the "half-dead could be seen staggering one on top of the other."[3] The rate of death prompted this famous physician to get out of Rome quickly, retiring to a country estate in Asia Minor until the danger receded.

Fast forward to the year 2020, which will be remembered as the year the world came to a stand-still, with nation after nation shutting their international borders and restricting travelers from coming into their country except for their returning citizens, city after city declaring a lockdown with only "essential services" allowed to operate. The once-golden pride of human achievement, the ability to easily zip around the world, stopped. The global travel industry, from flights to cruises, all came to a screeching stop, all because we had been invaded by this enemy.

Statistically, Covid-19 has shown itself to be much more destructive among older people than younger people, except for young people who suffer from a preexisting medical condition such as hypertension or lung, kidney, or heart disease. And most of these younger people are from racial minority communities. Additionally, essential workers from minority communities are more likely to need public transportation, most likely to live in intergenerational households, and less likely to have access to primary care doctors and health insurance.

Around the world, and the United States in particular, so far, the virus's impact seems to be concentrated amongst socioeconomically poor communities, where the number of deaths is triple the number of their socioeconomically privileged peers.[4] From states like Louisiana, Mississippi, Alabama, and Georgia, to cities like Detroit and Chicago (south side), the virus has ravaged these communities that historically have been racially and socioeconomically disadvantaged. The virus seems to be advancing significantly amongst younger people who are not only suffering economic disparity but health disparity as well. With how much things are unraveling, it points toward a future with many social

---

3. Ibid, 85.
4. Newkirk II, "Coronavirus's Unique Threat to the South."

disruptions, economic chaos, and an increased political fear of the other. This pandemic could feed the flames of violence, while at the same time it begs for an immediate and comprehensive response. The crisis presents us with a possibility, with a long-term plan to shift toward a more just and peaceful society, since Covid-19 does not discriminate. That being said, while the virus might not discriminate, the pandemic does.

There is a saying that droughts are God-sent but famine is man-made. Similarly, we are seeing that while the disease is a natural mutation, the pandemic is created and shaped by the policy of nations. Different nations with different policies are having different outcomes. I find myself thinking "the wages of sin is death" (Rom 6:23) but why are we BIPOC dying for sins of racism constructed by racist Whiteness? As we learned earlier by way of one of MLK's principles of social change, "the nonviolent resister has deep faith that justice will eventually win. Nonviolence believes that God is a God of justice."[5]

As we take steps to liberate ourselves from Covid-19's domination, we will need to develop a culture of peace and nonviolence as an antidote to the plague. King said half a century ago that it is either "nonviolence or nonexistence."[6] King's comments should prompt us to envision and work toward building a nonviolent world, or we will cease to exist.

In a time where some seek to combat this pandemic by clothing themselves with racism, xenophobia, and nationalism, steps need to be taken for humanity to overcome and survive it successfully. This would require a comprehensive, nonviolent approach. So, when the people of China, Italy, Spain, and the United States, and cities around the world, join in using the radical approach of social distancing, staying home for weeks on end, they are not only protecting themselves but protecting humanity in general, which is a nonviolent approach to fighting the pandemic.

Such a nonviolent approach does not guarantee a painless sacrifice, since we find ourselves in a state of disorientation in

---

5. King, *Stride Toward Freedom*, 15.
6. King, *Stride Toward Freedom*, 16.

the face of this pandemic which has taken countless lives. This nonviolent approach is increasingly needed to scale down the emerging catastrophe, and as such is an act based in love, not hate.

Covid-19 has exposed the systemic inequality that race and socioeconomics have on the daily realities of the poor and the marginalized in society. It shows how much easier it is for some people to deal with the crisis than others. Although various governments around the world, including the United States Congress, passed trillions of dollars in aid packages to help cushion the impact, I would say some of the governmental approaches can be akin to doing the same approach and yet expecting a different result. Most of the relief packages offered by the government have ended up in the hands of a few wealthy corporations.

The pandemic has been linked to an uptick in gender-based violence as country after country and city after city have reported an increase in calls related to gender-based violence as a result of either the quarantines or lockdowns imposed by cities or states. The Center for Global Development points to a number of factors that could fuel such acts of violence against women. These range from issues such as job losses, reduced income, food insecurity, fear of contracting the virus, exacerbated mental health, as well as disrupted routine. So, the more we take steps toward a full immersion in the spirit of nonviolence and healing, recognizing the importance of human connectedness and caring for one another, the more we will gather valuable lessons that will move society to a place where justice prevails in the fight against this plague.

PEACEMAKING IN THE MIDST OF A PANDEMIC

As a nonviolent practitioner, the immediate question that comes to mind is: How can we, in the midst of a pandemic, help people and communities shift their chaos (which, by the way, is chaotic, considering that nation after nation has gone on lockdown in order to interrupt the transmission of Covid-19)? With more people at home, preparing themselves for taking part in the next shift, it is key to ask the question: How? Instead of regarding the lockdown as some imprisonment, maybe we can envision a life of contemplation while in self-confinement, be it physical or spiritual. And in this posture, would you consider the cause for nonviolent way of life as, "nonviolence is a way of life for courageous people?"[7]

As we return back to pre-pandemic normal and continue to witness the reopening of city after city, there is an urgent call to engage in mobilizing a nonviolent army to go to war against the pandemic, despite the absence of a treatment, a cure, or a vaccine. This, even though the metaphor of "going to war against the virus" may sound antithetical to a nonviolence practitioner such as myself. I want you to be aware that my use of the metaphor comes from colleges' and universities' use of the term "war footing," as they try to assemble as much information as possible about any situation they seem to be fighting against. In the fight against Covid-19, states across the country have adopted a war metaphor to awaken society on the dangerous nature of the virus. beginning with New York's assumption of a stance of "war footing," with the intent to ready hospitals as the virus surges.[8] What does peace footing look like?

Peacemaking post-pandemic must include a multifaceted approach. We may have to look at operations where international communities work together, such as the kind of collaboration that happened after the Second World War. An example like that could help to rebuild communities and nations that have been adversely affected by the pandemic. Some areas of collaboration would include:

1. The international community must view the pandemic as of sufficient concern to intervene in, and must be willing to take the risks and bear the costs involved;
2. A plausible political agreement to define the general terms of involvement, since it would involve cross-border efforts;
3. Everyone must be prepared to accept the agreed-upon methods;
4. The international community must be essentially neutral as to how the pandemic would be treated and;

7. King, *Stride Toward Freedom*, 16.
8. Regan, "Wall Street Seeks the Right Metaphor."

5. The role as assigned to relevant agencies to address the wellbeing of all humanity must be the best universal practice.

A NEW WORLD COMING

I foresee a new social movement coming, one that would use the Covid-19 experience as a building block. Each of us is called to join this movement. It would be global and it would be a movement of movements. This movement has learned from previous campaigns, such as the Civil Rights movement in the United States and the quest for independence in countries like India and South Africa. This movement would be rooted in clamoring for justice, working for peace, and laboring for a new world that works for everyone. A new world is coming, like a hymn writer from the 1960s once said. The composer foresaw a new world vision coming as they faced the tumultuous decade of the sixties. It was a decade that saw the assassination of not only a president but a president's brother, as well as a civil rights leader. It was also a decade that included lunar landings, a decade of people rioting in the streets. It indeed appeared as if the world as people knew it was coming to an end. But on the horizon, the composer saw a vision of a new day that was about to dawn. This song echoes hope once again at a time when Covid-19 seems out of control. There is indeed a new world coming.

I invite you all to join me in embracing this new world of nonviolence as a way of humanizing society. Given that violence is increasingly becoming the main scourge of our time, how can we escape from the spiral of violence? We can do that by meeting violence with nonviolence that is effective in resolving conflicts. Taking a course in nonviolence would prepare you as you join the nonviolent army in support of this new world that is coming. So, are you ready? This is an invitation for you to consider committing yourself to becoming an agent of the dramatic system of transformation that is needed now more than ever.

In King's vision for integration, there is so much to learn about this new world and what is coming. In the "I Have a Dream" speech, King saw a vision of metropolitan boundaries uprooted, schools being integrated, transit and bus systems being desegregated, and all the boundaries of racial disparity done away with. This is a radically different vision than the existing conservative misappropriation, but with the advent of the pandemic, perhaps King's vision is ready to take off if we will only choose to look beyond the now and into the future.

EXISTENTIALIST MAN

A newspaper reports that eighty-seven people are burned to death in a New York City fire[9] allegedly because one man got angry with his girlfriend. Another says a thirteen-year-old boy does not want to see his father who has just been released from prison early on account of his good behavior. Why? Because his father poured kerosene around the bed where his then-six-year-old son lay, and set it on fire. The boy survived, but with third-degree burns.[10]

Almost everywhere we look, we see individuals and groups being treated inhumanely. We also see evil manifesting itself in the form of underserved illnesses we may not understand. I don't believe God uses illness to punish people for their sins; I do not think we feel pain because God is trying to teach us some sort of a lesson with the intention of bringing us in line. As the Bible reminds us, "the rain falls upon the just and the unjust."[11] What we can be sure of is that God is a God who loves us all the time. I believe God is a God who suffers with us, who feels our pain as we feel it. He strengthens us by giving us the peace and grace needed to overcome the pain life dishes out. In everything, his peace that transcends every understanding will guide and guard us.

That is why Jesus said, "Love your enemies," in his Sermon on the Mount (Matt 5). The question I am asking is: Is he serious, perhaps crazy, that we love our enemies? We may ask: Why should we do that? Why would He say that? The answer? So that you may be children of your Father in heaven. Then it even gets crazier: "Be

---

9. Blumenthal, "Fire in the Bronx."
10. Leonhardt, "Dave Rothenberg."
11. Matt 5:45.

Part I | The Three Conversions of Peter

perfect, therefore, as your heavenly Father is perfect" (Matt 5:48). I thought I had seen it all. What a tall order! Be perfect? It would seem that to make sense of this would be to understand that Jesus was also saying in this sermon that God, "makes his sun rise on the evil and on the good, and sends rain on the righteous and on the unrighteous."[12] What is this? God allows rain to fall and the sun to shine on both the good and the bad alike? You mean my God, your God, our God, is the God of those guys, too? You mean God is the God of the murderer, the unbelieving, the God of the sinners, the God of the liberals and the God of the fundamentalists? Surely, there must be some mistake here, Jesus! Not my God! Not your God! Not our God! You mean God is the God of all creation?

For the first hearers of these words, the enemy was more than a perception; they encountered the enemy every day. Some were religious leaders who called Jesus' followers heretics and heathens and stirred up riots against them. For the early Christians, the enemy was Rome, who insulted them, jailed them, and fed them to lions. Some of us have seen the enemy. They are the people who have hurt us. We do not live in an innocent world. All that happens to us is not necessarily the will of God or our responsibility. There might be people around us who have done us wrong and treated us unfairly; some of us can still hear the jeers and remember our tears.

Jesus and his disciples had just passed a man born blind from birth. For this man to have been born blind, the disciples asked Jesus, "Who sinned, this man or his parents?" (John 9:2). What kind of God did these disciples have? Did they think God looks down from heaven and says, "All right, fella, I know that you have been cheating on your tithes, your taxes, and your wife, and I am going to take that precious little baby in your wife's womb; I am going to strike that baby blind to punish you. That will show you, you little *fella*, how powerful and how able I am." What kind of God do some people have?

Of course, there are people who believe in a capricious God, a God who would strike a child blind because of the sin of his/her parents. This theological viewpoint finds its bearing in the

---

12. Matt 5:45.

Old Testament, but the words of the prophet Jeremiah help us to understand that God is not as capricious as some understand: "In those days, people will no longer say that parents have eaten sour grapes and the children's teeth are set on edge, instead everyone will die for their sin, whoever eats sour grapes their teeth will be set on edge" (Jer 31:29–30). Jeremiah was speaking of the coming kingdom; the kingdom that will come with the arrival of the Messiah.

Loving your enemy means seeing things from their perspective. It means understanding their hopes, dreams, and fears. It means taking the time to learn what is right from what is wrong, and what is wrong about what seems right, because we do not often know which is wrong and which is right. We cannot distinguish the good guys from the bad guys, although we often think we can but God's love is for the just and the unjust, so it makes it difficult for us to say with certainty.

When we hear the word "enemy," we are prone to think "bad guys." But "enemy" simply means "opponent." It does not connote good or bad, right or wrong. It means the person opposed, that's all. For God beams sunlight and releases the rain on the good and the bad, the righteous and the unrighteous. He doesn't indicate on which side of the divide we belong. God just treats us equally, without discrimination.

If we are to love our enemies, as Christ commands, we have got to see things from their perspective, which is from the other side, even if briefly. We have got to change our point of view and identify with a different character than usual. Think of the story of Joseph and his brothers. It is easy to identify with Joseph, but for the sake of loving our enemy, let us try to understand the position of the father and the brothers.

Joseph was Jacob's eleventh son, who was often referred to as daddy's boy. As one of the youngest, he must have whined a lot to get his attention. My youngest daughter is recognized by her siblings as daddy's girl. Their claim is that she whines and gets away with everything. We have recently moved homes and downsized, whereupon she got her two older sisters to share a room while she had a room to herself. According to her, she is going to be the last child to leave the home, so she needs her space. Could that be Joseph in disguise?

One day, Dad gave Joseph a colorful coat, so much better than anything the other siblings had ever gotten. That kind of gift must have caused some late-night conversation amongst the siblings. "Did you see what Dad did again?" Reuben asked. Judah, burning with anger, responds, "You mean that coat? I wish we all had something that new, so we can stay warm, keeping us safe from the cold nights out in the field." Genesis 37:4 says "they hated him, and could not speak peaceably to him." Now remember, we're identifying not with Joseph but with the brothers this time.

Young Joseph is a spoiled brat. He steals Dad's favor and tries to argue he has God's favor, too. Joseph has two dreams in which we, his brothers, bow down to him, he says, so we hate him more. Then he tells Dad of another dream, after which Dad scolds him, saying, "What kind of a dream is this? Shall we indeed come, I and your mother and your brothers, and bow to the ground before you?"[13] Our brother is an obnoxious seventeen-year-old and we have had enough. Let us plan to kill him. From the look of things, if we don't do this, he is going to wreck the family. But at some point, Reuben suggests we throw Joseph into a pit instead of killing him.

Joseph's brothers sold him to the Midianite traders passing by on their way to Egypt. He was taken down to Egypt, and Potiphar, an officer of Pharaoh, the captain of the guard, an Egyptian, bought him. But the Scripture account shows how the Lord was with Joseph (Gen 39:1–2a). With Joseph? The Lord with Joseph? What kind of God is this hanging out with slaves?

Next, Joseph worked his way up in Potiphar's household, winning his way up the same way he did with Dad. He got into a problem with Potiphar's wife and landed in prison. But Scripture says, in prison, "the Lord was with Joseph" (Gen 39:21). God's presence with Joseph shows a God who causes the rain to fall on the just and the unjust. "You have heard that it was said, 'You shall love your neighbor and hate your enemy.' But I say to you, love your enemies,

---

13. Gen 37:10.

bless those who curse you, do good to those who hate you, and pray for those who spitefully use you and persecute you."[14]

Real love is when you do good to a person who is doing evil to you. Now *this* is a special kind of love, I admit. The Greek language has four different terms that mean "love." I heard about a woman whose chickens got out of her yard into a neighbor's yard, which infuriated the neighbor. This woman was a godly Christian woman, but her neighbor was an ungodly man to whom she had witnessed many times without any success. This man just despised her. He despised Jesus, he despised the church, he hated the Bible, and he hated her chickens. One chicken got through the fence and this man picked it up, wrung its neck, and threw it back over the fence. She happened to be in the yard as the dead chicken landed right at her feet. Instead of reacting with anger and retaliation, the woman later went to ask this man if there was anything she could do to make things right with him so he did not have to kill her chickens. He was stunned by her calmness and the compassion extended to him, from that point on he stopped targeting her chickens.

When Martin Luther King Jr. began to stand up for the civil rights of Black Americans, many people who were filled with prejudice subjected him to incredible pains. His home was bombed. For thirteen years he lived under daily threats of death. He was accused of being a communist. He was stabbed by a member of his own race. He was jailed more than twenty times. Most of his sermons were written in jail cells. Yet, King said, "Love is the only force capable of transforming an enemy into a friend."[15] His understanding was that only divine love can indeed make that a possibility.

ROCKFORD STORY

In the late eighties, Black and Hispanic public-school students from Winnebago County, Illinois filed a class-action lawsuit against the Rockford Board of Education in the US District Court. The

14. Matt 5:43–44.
15. King, *Stride Toward Freedom*, 18.

Part I | The Three Conversions of Peter

plaintiffs, represented by People Who Care, asked the court for declaratory and injunctive relief, alleging that their constitutional rights had been violated by racial discrimination in the assignment of schools and classes to students in their school district.[16]

The story of West Middle School in Rockford (WMS) is similar to most schools in minority communities across the country. WMS had its own share of problems that led to the lawsuit titled "The People Who Care versus the Board of Education." This case threatened to split the city of Rockford between the haves and the have nots, between the White majority populace and the Black and Hispanic minority populace. As stated above, this began when the only high school in the Black and Hispanic community was closed, forcing students from these communities to travel across the city from the west side to the east side where another high school had been built, and causing the State Supreme Courts to intervene.

Despite the Supreme Court's intervention, the problems in the school continued. With rival gangs, food fights, and limited involvement by the school district, the problem the school faced persisted, reaching a point where it was further exacerbated by a city divided by race, socioeconomic class, and religious perspectives. Desiring to see peace and reconciliation restored to this school, first amongst students and then the community, I started by asking some religious leaders about their religions' practices concerning peace and how their teachings might be helpful in calming the anxiety faced by students and the residents from both sides of the city.

I decided to bring the different religious faith leaders together. My reason for doing this was for the purpose of bridge-building, to challenge them, "to remember the most powerful wells are invisible, in our minds. What might it mean to create a well in the midst of conflict, not a wall?"[17]

Peacemaking begins with changing the attitude of the individual toward conflict transformation, the way individuals look at conflict and how they respond to it. Such a view frames the individual's

---

16. People Who Care v. Rockford Board of Education, http://www.clearinghouse.net/detail.php?id=1052.

17. Porter, *Spirit and Art of Conflict Transformation*, 13.

response which could determine if peace can be attained or if the conflict will lead to destruction.

This story of WMS involves people who have chosen to intentionally work together in an active and direct way to address the conflict faced by the city of Rockford. Peacemaking that is backed up by religious leaders can prove to be successful in conflicts in the US and around the world, especially when religious leaders take the lead in building interethnic and interreligious peace among the faithful.

"Peace can include an inner, or subjective, journey towards what Judaism might call 'the eternal life' and Christians might call 'life in Christ' and Muslims call 'the surrendered life.' These phrases name a deeper and more complete side of peace, according to most world religions."[18] Radical peacemaking is an ongoing spiritual process that involves forgiveness, repentance, and justice, and which seeks to restore broken systems and relationships.

METHOD OF PEACEMAKING

Christians, who are not yet disciples of peacemaking, see conflict as a matter of paths. But as soon as they become converts to Christ's message of peace, only then does conversation about peace become normal. Therefore, the Christian approach to peace and nonviolence has benefited from the nonviolent part of the Jewish tradition. "In the first century, Jews were affected by the Roman Empire and longed for relief. As is frequent in such situations, the hope for someone to deliver them was high."[19] One man from Galilee, Jesus of Nazareth, offered a startling innovation; instead of military imagery, he offered an image of a suffering servant, which echoes what was said in the book of Isaiah 53, "conquerors would not be overcome by violence."[20] A counterproductive technique that could lead to calamity, it has, however, become the cornerstone for Christian peacemaking.

---

18. McDaniel, *Gandhi's Hope*, 78.
19. MacNair, *Religions and Nonviolence*, 106
20. MacNair, *Religions and Nonviolence*, 106.

PART I | THE THREE CONVERSIONS OF PETER

Jesus' response to the Roman Empire transforms the perception of "self, others and the issues in question."[21] There is no doubt that over the years, Christians have been actively involved in dialogues with other religions and community leaders as a way to achieve peace. In addition to this method, Christians in our community also use the act of listening as a means of reaching out to other faith traditions. These actions have created a pathway for talks that accommodated many different ways and opinions.

Listening has helped Christians prescribe the road that must be traveled on with other religions in order to attain peace. Imitating or repeating the teachings of Jesus in every action is part of the Christian mandate. Christian listening "involves a desire to walk in Christ's footsteps, day by day and moment by moment."[22]

Christian listening emphasizes openness and willingness to hear concerns from other faiths. It is a tradition that emphasizes humility and welcoming the stranger, both of which are defining characteristics of authentic Christian spirituality. As I understand it, listening to others and finding their personal experience is, in fact, a pathway Christians have used over time and throughout history to achieve peace.[23] In other words, it is seeking to always find God in the opposing party in the conflict.

Therefore, in Rockford, most of the Christians who have participated in this journey have continued to emphasize the need for openness and listening to others and their experiences. It is not just about listening, but carrying along the strangers who might even attempt to dishonor Christian wholesomeness toward peace. In the Rockford community, we (Christians) believe the contemporary Christian approach or effort of walking the way of peace between religions is a part of a larger voyage toward "a beauty that includes awareness of our interconnectedness."[24]

I worked with an interreligious group that equipped one another and the wider community with the skills of listening and

21. Lederach, *Preparing for Peace*, 18.
22. McDaniel, *Gandhi's Hope*, 39.
23. McDaniel, *Gandhi's Hope*, 39.
24. McDaniel, *Gandhi's Hope*, 38.

forgiveness. These are skills that are recognizable to Christians because Rockford was quite intentional in equipping people of other religions with these skills. As a result, people of different religions and atheists traveling on the same buses now share similar civic responsibilities. They are working and playing together, all for the sake of the good of the community. Among other things, what Christians in Rockford decided to do is educate people of other religions to understand what it means to a Muslim to "be a Muslim," and to a Christian to "be a Christian."

Christians in Rockford believe religious leaders and adherents must all embody these listening skills in their ways of living. Also, both adherents and their leaders must become the peace they commend to their world. Jesus riding on the donkey on Palm Sunday can be seen as an "ancient peace demonstration. The symbol had the king riding into the capital city of Jerusalem, but not on a valiant steed with swords blazing, but rather on a humble donkey. Palm branches rather than swords were in the hands of the crowd."[25]

I must confess that, down through the centuries, many Christians have had different ideas about God's grace. Many thinks of our relationship with God in terms of a law court and most of the confusion arises from the words "forgiveness" and "punishment." As a result of such a misunderstanding, the idea that God causes rain to fall on the just and the unjust seems to puzzle some.

QUESTIONS FOR REFLECTION:

- If we are able to build a lasting peace, how might society look before the next pandemic hits?
- How would this look to peacemakers?
- What are the forces working against the establishment of peace?
- What is the Kingian nonviolence antidote to that?

---

25 MacNair, *Religions and Nonviolence*, 109.

6

Tables in the Temple

Is There Such a Thing as Righteous Violence?

> "He overturned the tables of the money changers and the benches of those selling doves. 13 "It is written," he said to them, "'My house will be called a house of prayer, but you are making it 'a den of robbers.'"
>
> MATTHEW 21:12–13

> "Justice is love correcting that which revolts against love."[1]

ON SOCIAL MEDIA, AND most especially Facebook pages of people purporting to be Christians, I have come across some angry posts where they justify their use of strong language by pointing to the story of Jesus' cleansing of the temple. These comments usually are

---

1. Gabel, Peter. The spiritual dimension of social justice. *J. Legal Educ.* 673 (2013): 673–688

TABLES IN THE TEMPLE

a reference to a whip-wielding Jesus flipping over tables as he removes money-changers from the temple.

Mark 11:15 gives us an account of Jesus employing righteous anger to correct injustices happening in the temple. These injustices include the exploitation of the poor, the sale of animals for sacrifices at a high profitable rate, and money exchange; something of a modern-day currency exchange like Foreign Exchange (Forex) where, instead of giving a fair exchange rate, they use these currency changers to gauge travelers that had come a long way to offer sacrifice to the Lord.

Jesus' display of righteous anger calls us to act for justice. John's Gospel gives us a jarring image of an angry and violent Jesus, physically casting away people who were abusing the temple he loves and protects. It would not be wrong to say Jesus was unapologetically displaying righteous anger to prevent people from taking advantage of one another in the name of God.

In the story, Jesus is clearly irate. The reason the imagery is so powerful is the exact same reason it shouldn't be a default excuse for every angry rant expressed online or in person. This act was seemingly out of character for Jesus. The Gospels paint a picture of a Jesus who is consistent in practicing the kind of behavior he preached. Just as he told followers during the Sermon on the Mount to love their enemies and their neighbors as themselves, he praised the poor in spirit, the peacemakers, the merciful, and the meek.

Paul further qualifies the fruits of the Spirit Jesus talks a lot about, fruits such as "Love, joy, peace, forbearance, kindness, goodness, faithfulness, gentleness and self-control," and follows it with this line, "Let us not become conceited, *provoking* and envying each other" (Gal 5:22). When John tells us about Jesus grabbing a whip and throwing people out of the temple, people who were using the temple for their profit and gains, the story becomes powerful, because the Jesus we all have come to know preached peacemaking, not fighting. He preached patience and gentleness, not anger and violence.

If Jesus could get that angry, it was clear the offense committed must be an extremely grave one. The kind of behavior Jesus displayed in the temple that day is not by any means forbidden, but it was not exactly a daily part of Jesus' life either. The story remains powerful because it is an example of how we should reserve this type of action for rare occurrences in the face of injustice, not make it part of our regular lives. It should be so exceptional that when we display this kind of righteous anger, the people around us take note and respond in ways that are appropriate.

A Catholic priest in Dayton, Ohio was said to have recently defied his archbishop's order by denying communion to worshipers who did not observe dress codes; he had done that for many years, and it had gone unnoticed. The act of denying communion to anyone who is inappropriately dressed according to one's moral standard can lead to many questions. But finally, the archbishop had to step in. Whatever we may think of this priest's preference, we may think of it with shock or even anger; according to the Gospels, Jesus was angry as well.

He was angry when he was forbidden to heal on the Sabbath (Mark 3:5). Some instances of his expression of anger were implied. But when he came to the temple during Passover week, it was then his passion took over when he busted the money changers. The temple was a building that contains the holy of holies in which the high priest alone was allowed to enter, and this was done only once annually, on the Day of Atonement.

In the temple were many courts, including ones for gentiles, women, the Israelites, etc. Jesus' angry outburst took place in the gentile court. This court was always crowded; imagine the scene of the Notre Dame Cathedral in Paris, with tourists all over the place, sight-seeing. But instead of sight-seeing, there was buying and selling and exchanges of goods and animals. There was even a Forex table for travelers using different currencies as a precondition for sight-seeing. Many of the people in those courts came for the Passover, with a desire for a worshipful, prayerful experience. Instead of having that experience, however, they were confronted with the greed of the day.

"It is written," Jesus said to them, "'My house will be called a house of prayer,' but you are making it 'a den of robbers'" (Matt 21:13). It would be easy to assume his action was a wholesome condemnation of temple worship, but that is not so; Jesus regularly worshiped at temples. Jesus' anger was directed against those who exploited others and was against those who did so in the name of God and religion. Anger is not the opposite of love; it can often be the clearest expression of love.

As a generation, we are besieged by lies and lukewarmness when it comes to love. We are feeble as evil thrives under our noses. This evil is entrenched in our politics and customs, and it has the audacity to grow in the face of decency and justice. As Christians, we are often afraid to speak out or call out something that is wrong because we are afraid of what would be said about us but this should not stop us from pointing out things which are not right. Jesus cared so much and this resulted in his becoming angry when the religious leaders tried throwing roadblocks between God and the people.

WHEN IS IT RIGHT TO BE ANGRY?

I don't want you to think it is wrong for Christians to get angry. The story from an oceanside California robbery is worth noting. The would-be robber handed a note to the cashier demanding whatever cash she had. The woman reached for the cash drawer, then she looked again at the robber and the note he had just handed her. She pulled the entire cash drawer out, but instead of giving him the money she clubbed the robber over the head with the drawer. And again, and again. Money was flying everywhere and she kept beating him and shouting shame on him until the young man turned and ran away. Soon after that, the robber was arrested by the police.[2] Different people get upset at different things. There are times when all of us get angry. Sometimes the worst we can do is hold that anger in. What then should make us angry? The anger that Jesus displayed was focused on the injustices which were happening in the temple.

---

2. Roberson and Wallace, *Family Violence*, 21.

Part I | The Three Conversions of Peter

ANGER CAN BE CREATIVE AND CONSTRUCTIVE

Most of the social ills that have plagued humanity have been eliminated because someone got angry. One person with a cause can make a significant impact in the world. The twenty-first century will surely be one of continuing social, economic, and political turmoil and challenge, at least in its early decades, with the global call to address issues of race and racism. As I write this chapter, our current collective rage and anger against racism could lead to transformation in many sectors of society.

But it is equally important to acknowledge that many police departments across America are responding to the anger displayed across the country and have begun to make concerted efforts to address racial profiling. Many have recognized this reality and are utilizing their own internal rules, regulations, and policies to prohibit it. Many departments have incorporated new policies into training. Some other departments have also committed to collecting data on all traffic stops, stop-and-frisks, and other routine police practices. But the unfortunate reality is racial profiling remains with us. Yet we are called to continue the work to undo racism even if we do not have a chance to resolve some new and looming problems.

THE REST OF THE STORY

Jesus overturning their money-changers' booths and letting animals run through the courtyard didn't endear Jesus to the temple establishment. What right did Jesus have to do what he did? They wanted to know who Jesus was. Was he the awaited Messiah? Only the Messiah could get away with such shenanigans. The religious officials asked Jesus questions. "'What sign can you show us for doing this?' Jesus answered, 'Destroy this temple and in three days, I will raise it up'" (John 2:19). They understood Jesus in physical terms, but in reality, he was speaking metaphorically. They told Jesus how long it took to build the temple—forty-six years.

Following Jesus' death and resurrection, his disciples remembered this encounter. Remembering his words, they knew Jesus was not talking about a physical building but of his death and resurrection. They understood Jesus wanted to get people's attention, and he did so through a display of anger. Sometimes it is good to get angry. Anger can lead to creative and constructive solutions. In Jesus' case, he wanted to make a point, which is that God is not found in a building. God is to be found in the fellowship of Christ's people.

Social media, and most especially Facebook, has enabled people to engage in ways few people could have predicted. While it has the ability to connect the world and maintain virtual relationships, it also carries with it very specific risks. All of a sudden, confrontation stops being uncomfortable and starts being entertaining. Provoking a strong reaction stops being a rarity and starts being a standard part of dialogue. Loving your online neighbors and enemies stops looking so loving. Taking out a whip and flipping tables has become the norm. Many people have ceased to be known for their love and now are better known for angry outbursts, often with an echo of the episode where Jesus used whip in the temple. Yes, the story of Jesus cleansing the temple does show that we are allowed to be angry, but the life of Jesus teaches us that anger is the exception, because peace should be the standard.

Now, back to Jesus. What had begun as a service to the worshipers had, under the corrupt rule of the chief priests, degenerated into exploitation and usury. Religion had become external, crass, and materialistic; the temple of God had become a "robbers' den" (Matt 21:13). As Jesus surveyed the sacred temple grounds now turned into a bazaar, he was appalled and outraged. The worshipful atmosphere that befitted the temple, as the symbol of God's presence, was completely absent. What should have been a place of sacred reverence and adoration had become a place of abusive commerce and excessive overpricing. The sound of heartfelt praise and fervent prayers had been drowned out by the brawling of oxen, the bleating of sheep, the cooing of doves, and the loud haggling of vendors and their customers.

Realizing the purity of temple worship was a matter of honor to God, Jesus took swift and decisive action. Making a scourge of cords, he drove all the merchants out of the temple. Yet Jesus was neither cruel to the animals nor overly harsh with the men. The uproar he created was contained enough not to alert the Roman garrison stationed around the temple.

We too are therefore called to be angry at injustice. Many times, in the past, I've complained that things weren't fair. Sometimes I was legitimately wronged. Grumbling about injustice doesn't make things just, and the ensuing hostility doesn't help us effectively address things that need fixing. You can't create positive change from a negative mindset. To do so, you have to heal any pain you have had before you can set out to heal the world. And you have to stop seeing yourself as a victim if you want to access your God-endowed power to make a change.

When you find yourself in this anger cycle, try to stop the never-ending story by asking yourself, "If I could act and move the needle just a little bit toward what I think is a better outcome, what would I do?" Maybe you'd write a letter to a state representative, volunteer your gifts and skills, organize an event, make a new friend. The need to protect something, whether that's yourself or something else, can often lead to a strong reaction. If this is the case, start with some empathy for yourself. You might not get things right the first time, but you deserve compliments for trying to learn and for moving on. Remember, you are not your anger. Nor is your anger permanent or fixed. You can reframe your story by taking actions like forgiving yourself if for some reason you think you have a part to play in the cause of the injustice. One positive side to anger is it can be an appropriate response to injustice. No doubt, anger played a useful part in social movements for equality during the Civil Rights movement, and today we see such anger raising awareness via the Black Lives Matter movement. Anger may also lead to better outcomes in business negotiations, as well as an increased motivation to right the wrongs we see in the world.

QUESTIONS FOR REFLECTION

We have just seen Jesus' buttons pushed to the limit with the act of defiling the temple, and we may say one of Jesus' pet peeves is when people have no respect for God and even the temple.

- What are some of your pet peeves?
- How does your faith play a role in your anger?
- Should we be angry at injustice that happens around us?
- What could be some constructive responses to anger?

PART III

The Highest Place
The Vision of the Promised Land

In the last days the mountain of the LORD's temple will be established as the highest of the mountains; it will be exalted above the hills, and all nations will stream to it.

   ISAIAH 2:2 (NIV)

CHAPTER 7: THE HIGHEST PLACE: FAITH IN METAPHOR AND IN ACTION

Objective: The Vision of Peace Is the First Step of Working for Peace

Whole schools of theology have been built, but on the understanding that the healed world is possible only in the end of days, when Jesus returns. Therefore, if the world is inherently broken and violent, what is the point of working for an idealized peace we will never achieve? To be a peacemaker is to be recognized as the child of God, doing God's work by recognizing the signs of conflict and the signs of transformation. Beyond the semantics, we can make a difference in individual lives with a gospel of peace.

CHAPTER 8: SWORDS INTO PLOWSHARES: TOOLS FOR VIOLENCE AND TOOLS OF PEACE

Objective: A Vision for Turning Tools of Oppression into Tools of Peace

We have witnessed fire hoses turned on protestors and dogs released to chase down children. The tools of the world can be used to make war, for oppression or for peace. It is the Christian vision that swords can be made into plowshares, the tools of violence reshaped in the hands of the potter and turned to good. In Rockford, we have witnessed a reform from policing the community to community policing that has brought a hard-won peace and sown the seeds for justice.

PART III | THE HIGHEST PLACE

CHAPTER 9: I'VE BEEN TO THE MOUNTAINTOP: BEGINNING THE MISSION TOGETHER

Objective: The Hope for Peace against All Odds

The history of peacemaking is a mountain range—Moses viewing the promised land from a mountain; Jesus in the mountain refusing a cheap peace in exchange for worshipping the devil, Martin Luther King Jr. preaching a hopeful future for racial reconciliation. As we see the valleys and the mountains, we must be prepared for the long walk to a becoming a new community. When I first encountered a historic peace church, I thought they would have it figured out and be united in their mission. Instead, I found they were like the rest of the world, striving to articulate their values, seeking unity in the midst of conflict, and longing for a community of greater love. I also found there a reading of Scripture that believes in peace against all odds and an insistence that peacemakers can overcome obstacles to journey together.

7

The Highest Place

Faith in Metaphor and in Action

"Many peoples will come and say, 'Come, let us go up to the mountain of the LORD, to the temple of the God of Jacob. He will teach us his ways, so that we may walk in his paths. The law will go out from Zion, the word of the LORD from Jerusalem. He will judge between the nations and will settle disputes for many peoples They will beat their swords into plowshares and their spears into pruning hooks Nation will not take up sword against nation, nor will they train for war anymore.'"

(ISA 2:3–4)

"Peace cannot be kept by force. It can only be achieved by understanding."[3]

—ALBERT EINSTEIN

---

3. Lak, Political History of the World," 643.

Part III | The Highest Place

The vision in Isaiah 2:1–5 of nations streaming to Mount Zion in the last days, to come and to be instructed in Yahweh's Torah, is one of Isaiah's prophetic description of God as the universal Judge. As a Judge, he will issue decrees, exercising authority over the earth from above Mount Zion, "the mountain of the Lord's temple will be established as the highest of the mountains; it will be exalted above the hills and all nations will stream to it" (Isa 2:2). The mountain concept appears twice in the Pentateuch (the first five books of the Bible).

This prophecy, also occurs in another prophetic book of the Bible but with a slight variation from the one found in the book of Micah:

> Many nations will come and say, "Come, let us go up to the mountain of the Lord, to the temple of the God of Jacob. He will teach us his ways, so that we may walk in his paths. The law will go out from Zion, the word of the Lord from Jerusalem. He will judge between many peoples and will settle disputes for strong nations far and wide. They will beat their swords into plowshares and their spears into pruning hooks. Nation will not take up sword against nation, nor will they train for war anymore." (Micah 4:2–3)

However, Isaiah's seems to be cited the most, because of other prophecies by Isaiah regarding Christ and the fulfilment of the Messianic prophesies.

This prophecy predicts an end to political and economic oppression, as well as hateful and divisive ideologies. The nations will learn peace and will practice it.[4] This peaceful situation does not acknowledge the voluntary decision of humble nations as such, but a testimony to God's word that can compel nations to bring about peace, through His worldwide rule. This rule would compel all the nations to live in peace and walk in his ways.

Isaiah's prophecy begins with the description of Yahweh, the universal Judge, who issues decrees and exercises authority over the earth from atop Mount Zion. This could be depicted as

---

4. Brueggemann, *Isaiah: 1–39*, 25.

the pilgrimage of the nation of Israel's journey back to the promised land. The prophecy states that nations will one day beat their swords into plowshares, their spears into pruning knives, and that one nation will not take up its sword against another nation, all in all ceasing to learn about war. On the one hand, we encounter the texts which are in favor of segregating Israel and the nations, and on the other hand, these are texts which are in favor of the inclusion of foreigners into the community.

So, Isaiah's prophecy came during the stormy period at the period of the expansion of the Assyrian empire and the decline of Israel. At that time the Assyrians were sweeping westward into Aram (Syria) and Canaan. At about 733 BC, the kings of Aram and Israel tried to pressure Ahaz king of Judah into joining a coalition against Assyria. Ahaz chose instead to ask Tiglath-Pileser for help, a decision condemned by Isaiah. Assyria did assist Judah and conquered the Northern Kingdom in 722–721 BC.

The visit of the Babylonian king's envoys to Hezekiah set the stage for this prediction. Although the fall of Jerusalem would not take place until 586 BC, Isaiah assumes the destruction of Judah and proceeds to predict the restoration of the people from captivity. God would redeem his people from Babylon just as he rescued them from Egypt under the pharaoh. Isaiah predicts the rise of Cyrus the Persian, who would unite the Medes and Persians and conquer Babylon in 539 BC: "Who has stirred up one from the east, calling him in righteousness to his service? He hands nations over to him and subdues kings before him. He turns them to dust with his sword" (Isa 41:2). The decree of Cyrus would allow the Jews to return home in 538/537 BC, a deliverance that prefigured the greater salvation from sin through Christ. These events took place about 700 years before Christ was born. This clarion call that went out—the call which was heard by those paying attention, as it rang through time—this call says "he shall judge,"[5] or he shall exercise the office of a judge, or umpire. This reference was pointing to the God of Jacob (Isa 2:3). It is very clear he will do it by the Messiah, or under his reign.

---

5. Isa 2:2.

Part III | The Highest Place

This judge is to decide controversies; to put an end to all litigations and every form of evil that leads to war. By doing so, he will promote peace. The connection from this passage shows it simply describes what the Highest of All Mountains is all about. Nations that were once enemies shall be brought to peace by the influence of the reign of the Messiah, and this shall come about as these warring nations beat their swords into plowshares. In other words, the influence of the reign of the Messiah who would act as the Judge from this highest mountain shall put an end to all wars.

For upon this mountain, he shall show them the evil of all wars, and by disapproving of wicked passions which cause wars, he will promote peace. This piece of Isaiah's prophecy was picked up in the teachings of Jesus. And following predictions like these, the Messiah is called the "Prince of Peace"[6] and it has been and continues to be said that, "His peace shall not have an end,"[7] which means, as it was, so will it be today, tomorrow, and forever.

The prophet Isaiah uses semiotic imagery as a vivid reminder of the signs of the times, calling his listeners to recognize that the changes happening in the present can be understood by resigning the mountain metaphor as a place where lasting peace can be found. Hence, as the prophet says,

> See, the Name of the Lord comes from afar,
>   with burning anger and dense clouds of smoke;
> his lips are full of wrath,
>   and his tongue is a consuming fire.
> His breath is like a rushing torrent,
>   rising up to the neck.
> He shakes the nations in the sieve of destruction;
>   he places in the jaws of the peoples
>   a bit that leads them astray.
> And you will sing
>   as on the night you celebrate a holy festival;
> your hearts will rejoice
>   as when people playing pipes go up
>   to the mountain of the Lord,

---

6. Isa 9:6.
7. Isa 9:7.

THE HIGHEST PLACE

> to the Rock of Israel.
> The Lord will cause people to hear his majestic voice
>   and will make them see his arm coming down
> with raging anger and consuming fire,
>   with cloudburst, thunderstorm and hail.
> The voice of the Lord will shatter Assyria;
>   with his rod he will strike them down.
> Every stroke the Lord lays on them
>   with his punishing club
> will be to the music of timbrels and harps,
>   as he fights them in battle with the blows of his arm.
> Topheth has long been prepared;
>   it has been made ready for the king.
> Its fire pit has been made deep and wide,
>   with an abundance of fire and wood;
> the breath of the Lord,
>   like a stream of burning sulfur,
>   sets it ablaze. (Isa 30:27–33)

In this imagery, he makes full use of the metaphor in his denunciation of idols found in 44:9–20. "Do not tremble, do not be afraid. Did I not proclaim this and foretell it long ago?" (Isa 9:7). The mountain here is a mixed metaphor, simultaneously signifying greatness and encouraging people to wonder at how much greater the mountain of the Lord must have been. The prophet displays a mode of communication utilizing "both verbal and visual signs."[8] As followers of Jesus, we must go one step further in analyzing how and if the mountain imagery could still be relevant for our time. The prophet's use of the plowshare metaphor simply means they shall change their tools of war into tools for peace. They shall abandon the pursuits of war for the pursuit of peace. A spatial use of orientation metaphor—up and down, in and out—signifies the change which can happen when peace is pursued.

The Syrian plow, which was probably used in the surrounding regions, is a simple frame, and commonly so light that a man of moderate strength might carry it in one hand. Volney states that, in Syria, "it is often nothing else than the branch of a tree, cut below a bifurcation, and used without wheels. The plowshare is a piece of

---

8. Downing, *Changing Signs of Truth*, 25.

iron, broad but not large, which tips the end of the shaft. So much does it resemble the short sword used by the ancient warriors, that it may, with very little trouble, be converted into that deadly weapon; and when the work of destruction is over, reduced again to its former shape, and applied to the purposes of agriculture."[9]

Their spears were made of wood, with a sharpened piece of iron or other metal attached to the end. The pruning-hook, made for cutting the limbs of vines or trees, is, in like manner, a long piece of wood with a crooked knife attached to it. Hence, it was easy to convert the one into the other.[10]

Pruning-hooks (long knives for trimming vines) in this case means anything employed in reaping or mowing, such as a sickle, or a scythe, or any instrument used for cutting, including, a pruning-hook. These figures, as images of peace, are often used by the prophets. Micah 4:4 has added to Isaiah's description of peace as, "Everyone will sit under their own vine and under their own fig tree, and no one will make them afraid, for the Lord Almighty has spoken."

THE MOUNTAIN:

Mountains are a wonderful metaphor for the conflicts and the brokenness we encounter in life, and for the way we meet them. Mountains can also be a metaphor for the many opportunities and possibilities that come our way, and for the ways we take advantage of them. When we climb mountains, we sometimes have to face our deepest fears and find ways of overcoming them. In doing so, we get to know ourselves better, but we also learn more about our potential, what we could do if we really put our mind to it.

On mountains, we have to learn new skills and new knowledge to be able to move safely and enjoyably. For example, we have to learn to read the terrain, just as we have to be able to understand what's happening in the world around us. And we have to learn to cooperate with, and trust, others, because on the mountains our

---

9. Volney, *Ruins*, 189.
10. Volney, *Ruins*, 189.

lives sometimes depend on this ability. On mountains, we see new horizons and new summits, and we are able to look at the world from new viewpoints, enabling us to see completely new things or to understand things as we have never understood them before.

The Bible is full of references to mountains, how we ought to look to them, how God moves them, how they melt in his presence, or shake in his glory. God speaks to people on mountaintops, bushes burn, internal battles are fought. Tectonic plates are holy ground. At the mountain we find reconciliation and restoration of all things, on the mountain is the new humanity, in accordance with Scripture: "Therefore, if anyone is in Christ, the new creation has come: The old has gone, the new is here" (2 Cor 5:17). This new sense of being is both concrete and metaphorical and it's brought about by Christ Jesus. This is why reconciliation is an ongoing work of redemption of all things.

However, getting to the summit of the mountains is not without obstacles. We are a new creation, but so long as we are on this side of eternity, mountains will always be a part of our lives. Some of the obstacles one encounters on a physical mountain can be transposed into the spiritual realm as well. Much like the payoff after a period of hardship, or the completion of a long-term goal, the effort of climbing a mountain gifts an emotional feeling which you literally cannot manufacture any other way.

Mountains give so much to us (when you reach the summit, plant a flag, etc.), giving one a sense of accomplishment which goes beyond words, and so it is when one sees a once-broken relationship mended, communities that were in conflict are now living peacefully together, a fulfillment of promise of the lion and the lamb lying together.

> Righteousness will be his belt and faithfulness the sash around his waist. The wolf will live with the lamb, the leopard will lie down with the goat, the calf and the lion and the yearling together; and a little child will lead them. The cow will feed with the bear, their young will lie down together, and the lion will eat straw like the ox. The infant will play near the cobra's den, and the young child will put its hand into the viper's nest. They will

neither harm nor destroy on all my holy mountain, for the earth will be filled with the knowledge of the Lord as the waters cover the sea." (Isa 11:5–9)

When Jesus took three of his disciples—Peter, James, and John—and led them up a mountain to be alone with him, they were about to experience something unique. As the men watched, Jesus' appearance was transformed. His clothes became dazzling white, and Moses and Elijah appeared and spoke with him. At this, Peter, the boldest of the three disciples, offered to build three shelters, one for each of Elijah, Moses, and Jesus. Lest we think Peter had some special direction from above that caused him to say that, the Bible tells us he said it only because he was so frightened he didn't know what else to say! How relatable does Peter become to us when it is put that way?

The transfiguration of Jesus Christ on the mountain was a powerful demonstration of his divine nature and manifestation of his glory. As followers of Jesus, we are invited into this journey of imagination, of working for peace and reconciliation, of physically and metaphorically bringing the kingdom of heaven into our communities, of bringing into existence Jesus' prayer for peace in his Sermon on the Mount. "Blessed are the peacemakers for they shall be called the children of God" (Matt 5:9), captures the essence of his ministry and message. Reconciliation and peace lay at the center of God's nature and activity. "While we were still powerless, Christ died for the ungodly" (Rom 5:8). Forgiveness is rarely, if ever, deserved, but always necessary. It's a sign of the kingdom come finding expression in the kingdom now. It's a new creation reality coming to earth as in heaven.

QUESTIONS FOR REFLECTION:

- Have you had a mountaintop experience?
- Did that experience change your perspective?
- What would you want others to take from that experience?

8

Swords into Plowshares

Tools for Violence and Tools of Peace

HEALING OFFERED TO THE AGGRESSOR:

The disciples have heard Jesus say to them, "love your enemies," knowing how difficult that could be and that they might not even want to do it. So, while Jesus was praying in the garden of Gethsemane, Judas was hiding somewhere away from his fellow disciples. Matthew and Mark concur that a "crowd" accompanied Judas for Jesus' arrest (Matt 26:47; Mark 14:43), and Luke adds that "an officer of the temple" (Luke 22:52), that is, the Jewish temple police, were also present. John identifies these as the "officers from the chief priests and the Pharisees" (John 9:12).

The temple police could have arrested Jesus themselves, but since they had failed on a previous occasion when the Pharisees sent them (John 7:32, 45–47) the Pharisees this time sought Pilate's help with the Roman cohort which was present during all the Jewish feasts to help keep the peace. After waking his disciples (Matt 26:46; Mark 14:42), Jesus walked toward those who came to arrest him, for he knew of the plot against his life (John 6:64; 13:1, 3, 11, 18) and that his hour had come. Jesus could have evaded capture as he had done numerous times before, though perhaps he had not so much evaded capture in the past as evaded being made a king (Luke 4:30; John 10:40; 11:54). But he did not want to escape his destiny; he came to fulfill it. So, he voluntarily submitted to his enemies. As Dr. King would say, "there would come a time for which every man must decide whether he will walk in the light of creative altruism or in the darkness of destructive selfishness"[1]

In today's culture, selfishness is an evil that has taken root and it varies from person to person, often based on their experiences and relationships. In my own experience and observations, I have seen a correlation between faith and selflessness. Though they do not directly affect each other, I have seen that an increase in faith can lead to an increase in selflessness. I consider Jesus' act a call for people of faith to be selfless, even if it means to heal the aggressor as a way of making peace, as Jesus demonstrates for us in the garden by healing one of his captor's ears.

I was once walking through the middle school where I had volunteered as a lunch peacemaker one morning. As I walked past the front office, as I did every day, I stopped a little further down the hallway. I had a sense of God speaking to me, and it was never really an actual voice but more of just knowing what he was saying. I knew he wanted me to go back and simply tell the woman at the desk that I hoped and prayed she would have a great day. That seemed almost insignificant and silly, but I couldn't shake the feeling I got, knowing that this woman has been one of those administrators that saw us as intruders rather than helping to restore peace to this broken school. As I walked further away from that lobby, the sense was so strong I turned back and walked toward the door again. She was looking at her computer screen and didn't notice me pass for a second time. I wasn't, and am still not the type of person to approach someone else to start a conversation based on what I am sensing. To start a conversation is easy for me, but to tell someone what I feel God is saying is difficult and a different thing altogether. But I knew I just

---

1. Ricard, *Altruism*, 21.

had to do it, no matter how much I didn't want to. And so, I walked toward the lobby and stopped in the doorway. Looking up, she gave me the sweetest smile. I got the words out before I could change my mind.Now, it is easy to just say, "Okay, that was nice and I see the connection to your faith, but so what? How does this fit into the story of Jesus healing the aggressor?" The reason I am sharing this is simple. I had to stop worrying about myself and how I would feel and what I wanted. Instead, I was obedient and ended up doing something good not only for myself but for my new friend who was struggling with this job. Another point here is that I had the opportunity to be selfless. I continue to learn to follow an altruistic path, which is always intertwined with my faith.

A few days after my encounter with the woman at the lobby, I was told she had written a memo which was ready to be sent. The memo's intent was to bar us from coming into the school simply to separate church and state although we were not proselytizing. So, in a way, my act of obedience to the nudging to say hello prompted her to cancelled her intent. My gesture of recognizing her humanity helped her see us as people who cared for the well-being of the students, teachers, and administrators. When you recognize inner peace, strive to teach others its lesson. Do not make anyone out to be adversaries, irritable people, or distant from you. Recognize that as your duty. Do not hesitate to step into unfavourable circumstances. Do not be co-opted by them. Allow your beneficence to spread from your inner light, without calling any attention to it. Then your blessings will prevail far and wide, and your actions will be raised to a higher mountain for peacemaking.

SCHOOLS AS A FORM OF CONTROL AND CONTINUING INJUSTICE VS. EDUCATION

In Rockford, this dynamic came into play around the issue of school desegregation. First a bit of history. Advocates seeking to desegregate schools in American cities such as St. Louis and San Francisco in the 1990s were surprisingly met with fierce resistance from communities and school boards. The three cases dealing with this issue have reached the Supreme Court this decade. The court has significantly limited the role of federal courts in reforming school districts by focusing almost solely on returning districts to local control as quickly as possible.[2]

"In response to these rulings, numerous school districts have successfully obtained findings of unitary status from district courts, thereby being relieved of all court supervision on issues relating to integration. In a number of desegregation cases, the lower court judge has tended to move rapidly in dismantling racism with little evidence that those plans succeeded, that the districts would stay desegregated, or even that the school system itself wanted to be freed from judicial control."[3]

According to Shannon Fisk, "one of the main reasons for this dismantling of school desegregation is that many segments of the American society have come to question the propriety and effectiveness of the efforts. Criticism of school desegregation litigation has three main bases."[4] As Fisk explains, the fact that desegregation is being questioned has harmed the benefits, proven by research, of desegregation. The critics argue that neither the harms of segregation nor the benefits of desegregation are as great as is often claimed by social scientists. Others question the methods used by the courts, arguing that their plans should be less comprehensive and should focus more on voluntary approaches. Most fundamentally, some question whether courts are the best institutional actors to address these issues, both in terms of the legitimacy and efficacy of such action. One of those school districts that needed to be desegregated was the Rockford School District (RSD).[5]

People Who Care v. Rockford Board of Education School District #205[6] was an attempt to further the desegregation of schools that began at the height of the Civil Rights movement. However, that process placed most of the burden on the backs of minority

2. Hendrie, "Settlement Ends St. Louis School Desegregation Case," 281.

3. Rosenberg, *Hollow Hope*, 45. This argument showed the gains achieved during the desegregation of schools as a result of the action taken by Congress.

4. Fisk, "Importance of Full Court Involvement," 3.

5. Fisk, "Importance of Full Court Involvement," 3.

6. Cyplick, "People Who Care v. Rockford School District."

children to enroll in white majority schools. The Rockford school desegregation saga demonstrated the necessity for federal courts to ensure schools are desegregated.

According to records from the Regional Historical Center, the *People Who Care v. the Board of Education* showed that the Rockford School District was first confronted with evidence of discrimination and opposition to that discrimination in the mid-1960s. Some efforts were made to desegregate in the 1970s, but those efforts failed because of opposition by many school board members, the ineffectiveness of state government to pressure RSD to comply with state law, the failure of the federal district court to oversee the district's actions, and budgetary constraints. "The record further shows that the initiation of the People Who Care litigation led to some progress but there was evidence that the Rockford School Board was not fully compliant."[7]

Ever since these findings, however, the courts have been able to craft remedies that are successful in overcoming the opposition. This lawsuit, which was filed in May 1989, not only attacked the 1989 Reorganization Plan, but also, "alleged that the school district historically had engaged in a pattern of intentional segregation and discrimination on a system-wide basis. The court's decisions can be forcedly implemented; however, it does not often bring the systemic change that needs to take place."[8]

Twenty years have passed since the case involving *People Who Care vs. The Board of Education*, an issue that began after a meeting of concerned minority community members. The lack of transformation has prompted the community to explore peace between racial groups based on shared religious components and values. The phrase "people who cared" stuck and was uttered across Rockford for decades "in celebration and frustration as the city's failures to provide quality education for all students became exposed and battled through a race discrimination lawsuit filed on behalf of the group in May 1989."[9]

7. Cyplick, "People Who Care v. Rockford School District," 28.
8. Cyplick, "People Who Care v. Rockford School District," 28.
9. Cyplick, "People Who Care v. Rockford School District," 29.

Despite all of these changes, racial, religious, and socioeconomic disparity continued to exist within the school district. Based on the court's implementation, the question being asked was: Are the court's applications working? If not, why? And how can the Abrahamic faiths help bring desegregation to the Rockford schools?[10]

This situation prompted a group of leaders from the Abrahamic faiths to mobilize and organize the Center for Nonviolence and Conflict Transformation, and to work toward putting racial, religious, and socioeconomic disparity to rest. But the questions that arose were: How are we going to do that? How will we know that our goal as a group is being achieved? The leaders and I examined the historical situation and initiated an interfaith dialogue with a goal of bringing transformation. More importantly, we articulated some religion-based foundations for carrying out this dialogue. While we "emphasized the deliberative, formal, and theological nature of interfaith dialogue, distinguishing it from everyday religious encounters and conversations, our notions of dialogue varied."[11]

For example, some "Christian notions of dialogue stress religious witnessing, which is more than a verbal act; it is the co-witnessing of each other's faith for mutual growth and enrichment. Witnessing indicates a deeper engagement involving a more spiritual experience than just information gathering."[12] Knowing well that these religious dialogues are not immune to the effects of globalization, such an understanding prompted "these leaders to see the whole world as a community of humanity with a shared, physical space."[13] However, globalization posed a few challenges for this group in Rockford. Questions arose from some adherents of these religions regarding the text of Scripture to be used as a basis of our reconciliation. As a group, we agreed the faith of each religion could be articulated and explored through a discussion of texts that would build unity for this work.

10. Curry, "People Who Care."
11. Mackenzie et al., *Getting to the Heart of Interfaith*, 76.
12. Kayaoglu, "Preachers of Dialogue," 147.
13. Kayaoglu, "Preachers of Dialogue," 145.

These forms of engagement, in which the different texts of Scriptures from these traditions were discussed, created ways of allowing faith to be central in our work together. Participants were not pressured to come to agreement or consensus, so differences and questions were as welcome as similarities and differences. Sometimes these questions were left open-ended in the interest of putting into practice each group's faith practices. Even though the practices are preached separately, we could choose to put them into practice corporately.

Agreeing upon a shared understanding of avoiding proselytization of each other made it easier to build a working relationship. Another shared value is the sovereignty of their holy scripture, with each party adhering to his scriptural understanding as a guide for the application of the Golden Rule. Each adherent of these faiths should not view the others as outsiders but as bringing a rich tradition that could be helpful to peacemaking and conflict transformation.

PLANNING FOR ACTION

I assigned participants leaders from the Abrahamic faiths to read the books *Kingian Nonviolence and Leadership Development* and *Stride toward Freedom*. While discussing the books, several of the participants expressed concern about the difficult experiences of the Civil Rights movement and the racial segregation that had taken place. However, they were hopeful at the same time as they were able to read how different faith leaders were instrumental in helping to organize the passing of the Civil Rights Act of 1965.

Despite the prevailing racial attitude of the Rockford School District, the participants began to see themselves, the community, and the world in new and challenging ways. Over the subsequent months, the group continued their conversation, leading to the adoption of the school from which the civil lawsuit originated. They volunteered as a group, restoring programs that were no longer offered due to budgetary shortfalls. After-school programs offering reading, math, gardening, cooking, and much more were restored and staffed by volunteers. Through this new partnership, the worldview of Rockford began changing. Participants no longer saw each other as religiously different, but saw their goal of unity as the primary focus. And obviously, friendships were built just as bridges were built across religious lines. This was expressed in the sharing of meals together, caring for each other's well-being, and loving one's neighbor.

Working together in this manner is applicable to individuals as well as community groups focusing on developing a conflict transformation movement within their city. Many people are afraid of taking a step toward reconciliation because of the fear of the unknown. Small steps, like reading and discussing together, are very helpful. For this to happen, such steps need to take place in a participant's life before they choose to go on this journey of conflict transformation. Doing so means entering into a personal preparation phase and being open and vulnerable.

The old beliefs, patterns, and practices that seemed to have worked in the past may no longer fit. The old patterns of going it alone do not work. We remember what Jesus says in Matthew 9:16-17 about how one cannot pour new wine into an old wine skin, as it may cause a rupture of the old wine skin.

A different and new approach will be needed. I will call for the second order of change, which requires action steps not based on reactions. In this phase, the participant decides to do things differently. For example, instead of protesting against the school district, the participants choose to address poverty-related challenges at this school, like fundraising to provide school uniforms for all the students.

The third phase is what I call the transformation phase. In this phase, the participant's religious application of peace understanding is put into action. The practice of what is being preached in separate congregations is lived out. Although seen throughout the different phases, in this phase there is an actual sharing, in a public gathering, of how each participant's religion informed his or her participation in the school's transformation process.

FROM POLICING THE COMMUNITY TO COMMUNITY POLICING

Before the racial uprising which led to the formation of the Black Lives Matter movement, which was partly a reaction to the killing of young black men by police officers who purportedly were keeping and maintaining law and order, the conversation on community policing was more about policing the community rather than community policing. However, the concept of community policing is not new. Community policing philosophy has always been around. It is the philosophy that works at promoting organizational strategies that support the systemic use of partnerships and problem-solving techniques that are proactive to addressing any condition of public safety, such as crime, social disorder, and fear of crime.

Community policing is about integrating police departments more closely with the communities they serve. Residents and neighborhood groups are given a seat at the table to participate in developing enforcement strategies and goals. At the same time, relationships are established with partners such as local governments, nonprofits, and community health centers, which strongly require individual officers to become involved in and with neighborhood groups, including providing extracurriculars, most especially for at-risk youths. The judgment behind such actions is that when residents and officers interact outside the context of distress or arrest, they are more easily able to establish a baseline of trust and mutual respect.

Community policing has its roots in a set of principles set out by Sir Robert Peel, the UK Home Secretary who created London's Metropolitan Police in 1822.[14] Based on those objectives, I proceeded to invite my city's police department to train in Kingian Nonviolence for Law Enforcement, a strategy that was developed following the Civil Rights movement. Although it took a while to get a buy-in from the department to take this step, the department eventually agreed to take part in a two-hour, weekly orientation for six-weeks. I remember on the first day, most of the management

---

14. Brogden and Nijhar, *Community Policing National and International Approaches*, 13.

members showed up not looking enthused by the prospect of some civilian training them on nonviolence community policing.

Another challenge I was confronted with was that I was in the Black minority, trying to introduce the concepts of nonviolence policing to an overwhelmingly white management of the department. I had a backup, and the plan was having my white colleague introduce a general overview of our journey. And did I mention my training team consisted of three women? One Black, the other two White. Everything was looking less than promising. But on the first day, my white male colleague did a wonderful job of presenting an overview of what would take place in the next few weeks.

The training took off and by week three, I was asked by one of the deputy's chiefs: "Why hasn't such a training been incorporated into the police training?" Shocked to hear that question, I turned it back to him saying that the concept we were learning there could be institutionalized, and when they proved to be successful, we could become that national model for what community policing, as originally intended, could look like.

Training was offered to the command staff and management of the department. This community policing training became a model for a new form of partnership between the community and the police department, which helped bridged the gap that had previously existed, and which helped shift the dynamic from policing the community to community policing. Together we developed different concepts and models of how the policing culture had to change, first by looking at a joint project to equip at-risk youth with skills, while simultaneously building relationships with these at-risk youth. This progressed to having events like coffee with a cop, a cop reading for school children, or block parties that began with the slogan "Party with the Po-po."

There is an old proverb that says "the proof of the pudding is in the eating." I am writing this five years after the program of nonviolence community policing was introduced to our city. We have heard stories of success after success from officers working with at-risk youth who initially see the police as a threat but change their minds to see the police as an ally in their success, even to the point in some cases of having a dream of one day becoming a police officer themselves. Our city's police department has made summer block parties part of their program. They have also introduced geographic policing, where officers work in a specific geographic part of the town, building relationships with the community. The officer residency program is where an officer lives within the community as a neighbor who acts as peacemaker and mediator for their neighborhood.

Strong relationships of mutual trust between police departments and the communities they serve are critical to maintaining public safety and effective policing. It is so critical at this juncture. In the wake of many incidents involving police use of force, and other issues like racial profiling, the legitimacy of the police officers and their respective departments has been questioned in many communities. Cities across the United States experienced large-scale demonstrations and protest marches in the year following the incident where an unarmed black teenager was shot and killed on Aug. 9, 2014, in Ferguson, Missouri. And in some cases there have been riots over the perception of police misconduct and excessive use of force. In light of these incidences, I am advocating for robust nonviolent policing to be instituted as part of national police training. And not just during initial training, but also an annual refresher course would be offered, with a required certification in nonviolent policing as an expected result.

DOING RECONCILIATION

As Christ reconciled humanity to God, the "church proclaims and embodies the ongoing story of God's reign revealed through Christ."[15] If Christians, then, are called to be ambassadors of reconciliation, "the church has to be involved in an inward and outward journey of reconciliation."[16] The African concept of *ubuntu*[17] (humanness) is particularly compelling, described by Desmond Tutu "as a person with open availability to others, affirming of others and does not feel threatened by others."[18] "The religious dual legacy in human

---

15. Hartshorn, "Theo-Politics of Reconciliation," 23.
16. Déogratias, "Mercy in a Conflictual Society," 15.
17. Tutu, *No Future Without Forgiveness*, 43.
18. Tutu, *No Future Without Forgiveness*, 44.

history regarding peace and violence"[19] calls Christian discipleship to be intentional in resolving conflict as it arises, as taught by Jesus in Matthew 18. Conflict resolution theories, to an extent, have done some systematic examination of the "decision-making process of religious actors and leaders in order for strategies of peacemaking to be effective in the relevant contexts."[20]

Some conflict resolution theorists have argued that "the study of religion and conflict resolution will yield new information in their inquiry."[21] They also want to look at: (1) the struggle between intracommunal moral values and other traditional values that generate conflict, (2) multifaith or interfaith dialogue and pluralism as conflict resolution strategies, (3) the impact of religious leadership on conflict generation and resolution, (4) the limited scope of religious ethics in regard to the rejection of nonbelievers and traditional out-groups, and (5) the promising role of interpretation of sacred tradition in generating peacemaking strategies. The peace process can be a way of living and working. The peace process is an open-ended, multilevel political process of continuation.[22]

Lederach calls it a journey towards reconciliation when, "leaders and thinkers make a commitment to the value of peace, from classical texts to modern reformists. . . . Furthermore, these religious actors continue to play an increasing role in resolving conflicts domestically as well as internationally."[23] These "leaders have successfully intervened in and mediated conflicts in the United States, Africa, Asia, and Latin America. However, a faith-based commitment to peace can be a complex phenomenon,"[24] due to the fear and perception of one group proselytizing the other. While some believers "creatively integrate their spiritual tradition

---

19. Gopin, "Religion, Violence, and Conflict Resolution," 1–31.
20. Gopin, "Religion, Violence, and Conflict Resolution," 10.
21. Gopin, "Religion, Violence, and Conflict Resolution," 10.
22. Lederach, *Moral Imagination*, 23.
23. Jackson, *Classical and Modern Thought*, 23.
24. Jackson, *Classical and Modern Thought*, 23.

and peacemaking"[25] together, "many others engage it in some of the most violent places confronting the global community today."[26]

Conflict resolution practitioners work at "connecting the relationship between religion and conflict resolution strategies in the following ways."[27] Religion "plays a central role in the inner life and social behavior of millions of people, many of whom are actively engaged in the struggle for peace and justice,"[28] with a goal set toward reconciliation. The desire for engagement in the struggle for peace and justice calls for a serious theological conversation among faith communities. For Christians, reconciliation is both a divine act and a human responsibility. For the church, reconciliation is both a gift and a task. "Reconciliation is an ongoing spiritual process involving forgiveness, repentance, and justice that restores broken relationships."[29]

How then would you know when you have been successful? This is a question a member of my community group asked us as spiritual leaders. I was completely caught off guard by this question. I fumbled for an answer, but after a few tries I realized I was not giving a straight answer. This question haunted me for a long period and I continue to ask that question today.

However, after years of being in the trenches, I think I am ready to give my sense of what I think is the answer. My questioner was looking for a physical answer to show success, but from a Christian vantagepoint, spiritual and moral values guide our intended outcome, and so cannot easily be measured by the same metrics and material success.

Reconciliation is truly a journey, not a destination, it is a process that leads to personal, spiritual, social, and systemic transformation, and it is a mystery that can only be discovered. So, in a nutshell, reconciliation is a nonlinear process for measuring progress. Reconciliation is experience through different phases in

---

25. Jackson, *Classical and Modern Thought*, 23.
26. Gopin, "Religion, Violence, and Conflict Resolution," 12.
27. Deutsch et al., *Handbook of Conflict Resolution*, 121.
28. Deutsch et al., *Handbook of Conflict Resolution*, 121.
29. McNeil, *Roadmap to Reconciliation*, 65.

one's life. But the lack of a metric for success make its all the more fulfilling with an "Aha!" moment once that is experienced.

In my personal journey, I have arrived at the following fundamental skills to stay the course. To help you to be ready for reconciliation, and if you want to be successful, I have drawn up these six basic skills that are essential for the road to reconciliation, they are;

- Gathering of Information
- Reflection
- Building community
- Listening skill
- Problem solving skill
- Conflict reconciliation skill

First you have to learn how to gather information that will enable you to identify the underlying condition with respect to what has been done before you and how you can respond. Next, you have to think of how to reflect on all the information you have gathered. This, of course, will follow after you have done some work processing the information you have gathered. Another needed skill is building the beloved community, a process which allows you to engage the community through active listening as together you distill the information that's been gathered. Lastly, you must develop the ability to problem-solve through conflict reconciliation. When all these skills are in place, then I would say you are ready as an individual or a community for reconciliation to begin.

QUESTIONS FOR REFLECTION

- What are some of the costs—for you and your group—of pursuing conflict transformation?
- What are some of the costs of not pursuing transformation?
- How do you see God at work in the art of practicing what you preach in your separate congregations?

9

I've Been to the Mountaintop

Beginning the Mission Together

"And after six days Jesus took with him Peter and James and John, and led them up a high mountain by themselves. And he was transfigured before them, and his clothes became radiant, intensely white, as no one on earth could bleach them."

MARK 9:2–3 ESV

"I've been to the mountaintop. And I don't mind. Like any man, I would like to live a long life. Longevity has its place. But I'm not concerned about that now. I just want to do God's will. And He's allowed me to go up to the mountain. And I've looked over. And I've seen the promised land. I may not get there with you. But I want you to know tonight, that we, as a people will get to the promised land. And I'm happy, tonight. I'm not worried about anything. I'm not fearing any man.

Part III | The Highest Place

Mine eyes have seen the glory of the coming of the Lord."[1]
Martin Luther King

The history of peacemaking is like a mountain range—Moses viewing the promised land from a mountain; Jesus in the mountain refusing a cheap peace in exchange for worshipping the devil, when being tempted by the Devil, Martin Luther King Jr preaching a hopeful future for racial reconciliation. As we see the valleys and the mountains, we must be prepared for the long walk to a becoming a new community. When I first encountered a historic peace church, I thought they would have it figured out and be united in their mission. Instead, I found they were like the rest of the world striving to articulate their values, seeking unity in the midst of conflict, and longing for a community of greater love. I also found there a reading of Scripture that believes in peace against all odds and an insistence that peacemakers can overcome obstacles to journey together.

NEW COMMUNITY, BRETHREN VALUES

I arrived in Rockford, Illinois, in the dead of winter, to start planting a church with the Church of the Brethren. Temperatures dipped below zero, making the adjustment to this change more difficult, considering I had just moved from Kona, Hawaii. The Church of the Brethren is an historically peaceful church. The early Brethren were heavily influenced by the Anabaptists and early Pietism movements happening in the late sixteenth century. As Carl Bowman wrote,

> "Alexander Mack's Brethren were heavily influenced by Southern German/Swiss Anabaptists, especially Mennonites with whom they have very close contact."[2]

These early Brethren embraced Anabaptist principles, which are:

1. a commitment to the unadulterated biblical doctrine;
2. devotion to the New Testament;

---

1. King, "I've Been to the Mountaintop," para. 4.
2. Bowman, *Brethren Society*, 5.

3. strong observance of the Lord's supper;
4. a commitment to nonviolent resistance;
5. not taking of oaths of allegiance to the state;
6. recognition of the church as a gathered community; and
7. a commitment to freedom in religious worship, etc.[3]

In sum, Brethren were molded by a radical Pietist understanding of spirituality as well as an Anabaptist understanding of the church in society.

BUILDING COMMUNITY AROUND SHARED IDEAS

Based on this history, I learned an important principle that has stayed with me. Contrary to popular belief and dependency on self-sufficiency, community stems from shared mission. It is not enough to just be friends or sit and hear someone's story, allowing yourself to feel genuine compassion for the other. These things are certainly helpful, but they are not enough to sustain a group over the long haul and bring a longed-for systemic change.

Being new in Rockford, I quickly realized the need for a community that is coalesced around a single mission, a mission that every member who decides to join the community will buy into and be on this mission together. This led to not only gathering people for worship on Sunday, but gathering a community of the Abrahamic faith family to be on a mission together. Soon we began a group called Rockford Partners for Excellence (RP4E). RP4E's mission was to address the challenges faced by the majority of middle schoolers in continuing their educational pursuits into high school. Despite our theological differences, we chose to focus our attention on this mission for our community.

I led the group to explore some existing practices of groups that had been able to build and grow together, in spite of their differences. We noticed successful groups contained diversity within them. Like United States military chaplains, who have a commitment to work together as diverse religious groups in spite

3. Bowman, *Brethren Society*, 5.

Part III | The Highest Place

of their differences, we chose to work toward a common mission. Our goal, unlike the military, is conflict transformation, and our mission is working together.

Our teammates might not be like members of a sports team, but our teammates are from the other religions of the Abrahamic family of faiths. Our main connection is our claim to Abraham as our father. Consider your favorite sports team. These teams are successful at building diverse communities because they are on a mission together. We too were on a mission together. We were on a mission to see transformation coming in our public schools' food fight and the arising conflict it created. I found that having this shared, common mission makes all the difference.

As we began preparing to be radical reconcilers, the story of Jesus in his birthplace, Bethlehem, as told in the Gospels, comes to mind. Today in Bethlehem, much of the commerce is focused on this claim to prominence. One can visit the Church of the Nativity, which is said to be built on the site of Jesus' birth. The Church of the Nativity today is encircled by a high barrier and security. Jesus of Nazareth set an example for his followers. He has demonstrated to the church what radical reconciliation is: to be open and welcoming. But what we see at the Church of the Nativity contradicts those teachings. Paul's call for a new humanity in Ephesians 2 is about a humanity that embraces both Jews and gentiles, a new, reconciled humanity in Christ that mirrors what Jesus lived. Jesus was the incarnation of reconciliation. The notion of Jesus as the same yesterday, today, and forever is central to our reclaiming of Jesus as reconciler. Jesus has much to say to us in the context of the exclusion and division that is seen in the twenty-first century.

Being on a mission together calls Christians in this group to model Jesus' inaugural sermon, declaring the good news for the poor and oppressed. Jesus often spoke in parables and his parables often contained rhetoric that was directed at power structures by shining the spotlight of the prophetic tradition on the injustices of the Roman occupation. We may not have a Roman occupation today, but the power structures in society are not very different from the Roman occupation of first-century Palestine. Not only did Jesus preach a message of reconciliation and social justice, he actually lived it. We too are called to live that out in Rockford in our work as a team on a mission.

The ministry of Jesus reflected the influence of his Galilean roots. Our team's mission in Rockford must reflect our Rockford roots. Members of our community should be able to read and reap the fruit of our work and see what true reconciliation looks like, or should look like. We started by meeting as Abrahamic faith leaders, hearing what hope and vision each of the group leaders has for reconciliation. Stories were shared around the table.

FINDING COMMONALITIES

I led the group to take time to do a historical study of Jesus, Muhammad, and YHWH, to remind the group about the mission each of these religions has with respect to peace and conflict transformation. Together we discovered the distinctions between Christians and the other Abrahamic faiths. Our discovery together showed "Jesus did not come from a wealthy, privileged background or from a family of high social standing with powerful political connections."[4] Jesus of Nazareth, the son of Mary and Joseph, was not of the hierarchical priestly class. But from his beginning, Jesus looked at the world through different eyes.

This significant development helped our group reorganize, finding a common mission as a team built around an open theological study that juxtaposed Judaism, Islam, and Christianity. We found a common ground as we worked to address the challenges our middle-school students were facing, especially our city's minority middle school students, whose graduation to high school rate was less than 60 percent.

To accomplish this, we set out to discover a deeper dimension of our faith journey, seeking to move beyond the five stages identified by Pastor Mackenzie, Rabbi Falcon, and Iman Rahman:

1. Moving beyond separation and suspicion.

---

4. Stegemann and Stegemann, *Jesus Movement*, 22.

2. Inquiring more deeply.
3. Sharing both the easy and the difficult part.
4. Moving beyond safe territory.
5. Exploring spiritual practices from other traditions.[5]

We worked through these stages one step at a time at the onset of our mission together, learning to know each other, building tolerance and bridges. And as we contemplated the meaning of the sacred in spite of these diverse views, such views became the beacon of hope for our work and the school community.

PRACTICAL PROCESSING

As you consider the five stages above, you may discover that you have already had similar experiences in a different place with different people. Do any of the steps stand out to you? We invite you to share what faith means to you with someone of another faith, not by way of proselytizing, but as a way of sharing your hope for a transformed world. Ask God for a radical understanding of what it means to be on a common mission, to be in mission with people from other faith traditions. Pray that you will be able to communicate better with each other.

BEGINNING WITH INTERFAITH DIALOGUE

Grace that is cheap has become the number one enemy of Christianity. Dietrich Bonhoeffer, in the book, "The Cost of Discipleship," describes cheap grace as "grace without discipleship, grace without the cross, grace without Jesus Christ."[6] The presence of cheap grace makes the Christian to retreat in the face of conflicts instead of engage. I am not advocating for a partial engagement, but a full engagement that may include a dialogue with other faiths, and as such, would act as a witness to those of other faiths.

---

5. Mackenzie et al. *Getting to the Heart of Interfaith*, 8.
6. Bonhoeffer, *Cost of Discipleship*, 45.

Paul demonstrates how to have a meaningful engagement in Acts 17, which tells us when Paul arrives in Athens, there were many Greek gods' citadel. In that city was the Areopagus, a place where a council of civic leaders met. This council had charge of religious and educational matters in Athens. As was his custom, he went to the synagogue and reasoned with the Jews and God-fearing gentiles. He also preached in the marketplace. But one of the many altars available caught his attention. On it was an inscription: "TO AN UNKNOWN GOD." In their ignorance, the Greeks had erected an altar to whatever God they might have inadvertently left out of their pantheon. Paul masterfully uses this altar as an opportunity to share with them about the one true God.

In today's context, interfaith gathering has become a place for such constructive engagement. But many such efforts get stalled after a few token meetings and a few initial forays into interfaith territories because people are at a loss. "I can see the time coming when people belonging to different faiths will have the same regard for other faiths that they have for their own."[7] The best place to begin is with one of the most influential peacemakers of the previous century, Gandhi. Was he right? Has the time come upon us when people of different faiths have the same regard for each other? I have doubts because of the rise of fundamentalism in America, Syria, Iran, Afghanistan, and Nigeria.

Yet, there are signs of hope, and often in surprising places. Consider the community market in Rockford. When we walk to the city market, we find people of different creeds and colors, filled with beauty. And if we look a little further, we see ourselves in the other, most of whom define themselves as seekers, as spiritual but not religious. Others among the religious seekers are religiously affiliated and often describe themselves as both religious and spiritual. Simply put, they belong to a particular religious community, be it Jewish, Christian, or Muslim. Their roots in this community give them wings to fly, but yet they are open to relating to the other religions.

---

7. Mackenzie et al., *Getting to the Heart of Interfaith*, 15.

All of this suggests that despite the rise of fundamentalism all over the world, a longing and need for hope and peace is apparently growing. At the interfaith council in Rockford, for instance, all religious participants sought to create space for other religions to feel welcome. It was a milestone for religious diversity as people holding these beliefs were offered the platform to express their convictions.

Of course, religious diversity is not something new. It has always existed and will continue to exist. In past practices, each of these diverse religions has stuck with its adherents' point of view on the subject of origin. Scholars, however, have disagreed on how religion began. This has become problematic because the Abrahamic faiths each have a claim to this historical beginning. We can also safely assume there have been various religions in the world that preceded the calendar we currently use. But there is something new about the practice of interfaith dialogue.

The degree and the scope of awareness has grown among these religions as a result of urbanization and globalization, creating a deeper understanding of each other's practices.

Christians draw great inspiration from Jesus' teachings that seem to welcome the other—as can be seen in his relationships with the Pharisees, Sadducees, and zealots who were always welcomed to join him for dinner. Jesus, through the Scriptures, could be said to be the first practitioner of interfaith dialogue, someone who not only ate with Jews but with gentiles as well, welcoming all of them into the conversation.

> Now the tax collectors and sinners were all gathering around to hear Jesus. But the Pharisees and the teachers of the law muttered, "This man welcomes sinners and eats with them." (Luke 15:1–2 NIV)

> "What then is the connection between Christian, Muslim, and Jewish nonviolence and Christian dialogue with other faiths?"[8]
> "Some Christians believe that true nonviolence is possible only for those whose lives have been shaped

---

8. Gopin, "Religion, Violence, and Conflict Resolution," 23.

by the example and sacrificial suffering of Jesus Christ. In practice, however, Christians have worked alongside Jews during the civil rights movement, with Muslims in the struggle against the Vietnam War, and with Jews, and Muslims in pursuit of peace in the Middle East."[9]

"Interfaith dialogue has become an integral part of nonviolence. But what exactly does it mean for Christians, as Christians, to engage in nonviolent social action alongside people of other faiths and ideologies? In the book, *Nonviolence for the Third Millennium*, G. Simon Harak, S.J., offers a wealth of materials from which answers to this question might emerge."[10]

Also, Walter Wink, in *Jesus and Nonviolence: A Third Way*, writes:

> The third way is not a perfectionist avoidance of violence but a creative struggle to restore the humanity of all parties in dispute.[11]

At the core of interfaith dialogue is a moving beyond separation and suspicion, for separation and suspicion can be subtle. They often crop up when least expected, in ways that disappoint representatives from other faiths and cause people to build walls between each other. Interfaith dialogue happens when there are shared vignettes. At the core of the interfaith journey is the ability to learn the foundations of another's faith, which can lead to a better appreciation of such traditions:[12]

> Familiarity with the classical sources might make it possible to distinguish where and when leaders are genuinely expressing their tradition in ways that express its core beliefs and practices.[13]

A balanced interfaith approach engages with multiple faith communities, seeking to transform the religious division that drives

---

9. Mackenzie et al., *Getting to the Heart of Interfaith*, 51.
10. Mackenzie et al., *Getting to the Heart of Interfaith*, 52.
11. Wink, *Jesus and Nonviolence*, 51.
12. Mackenzie et al., *Getting to the Heart of Interfaith*, 51.
13. Gopin, "Religion, Violence, and Conflict Resolution," 29.

conflict, which includes religious bias that stymies collaborative peacebuilding.

ACT OF PRACTICING WHAT WE PREACH SEPARATELY:

We may look similar but we are different

The relationship between Christians, Muslims, and Jews has been divided and shaky for millennia. These religions are locked into competing truths that have often led adherents to resort to force as a way of driving truth home. And yet, these religions proclaim peace as a core tenet of their faiths, and all claim to be the descendants of Abraham. This shows that the Abrahamic family, like any family, is made up of individuals who tell different versions of the same story. Often times, people who grew up in the same house, attend the same school, and travel to the same places together, perceive their experiences very differently. When you ask these members to share their stories and experiences, you will be surprised to find many points of discord in the stories. This is not because they want to disagree with one another, but it is simply a matter of individual semiotics. Robert Yelle defines semiotics as the

> discipline devoted to the systemic study of signs, symbols, and communication; it overlaps in its method and subject most directly with language and rhetoric.[14]

Therefore, despite the differences in the practices of faith expressions that exist amongst the Abrahamic faiths, they could see the potential for change in working together. Just like, when family stories are shared from different perspectives, it can lead to rage and anger or it can lead to a juicy session of storytelling. Like families, members of the Abrahamic religions continue to argue over who is the most entitled. My perspective as a follower of Jesus? The Christocentric approach has proven over time that Jesus is timeless.

---

14. Yelle, *Semiotics of Religion*, 1.

SIGNS OF CONFLICT AND SIGNS OF TRANSFORMATION

Conflict transformation has the power to build and also the power to tear apart and destroy people and communities. Understanding signs of what transformation could look like is helpful. What then are some signs of conflict and signs of transformation that one could find? One sign is a change of attitude toward conflict.

> Our transformation begins with our attitude towards conflict, the way we look at conflict and the way we respond to conflict.[15]

Adopting a constructive attitude and response toward conflict involves understanding conflict as something which is natural and sometimes necessary. Such an attitude is often referred to as the place where the rubber meets the road. It requires knowing the signs of conflict and transformation.

Conflict

As American society includes a growing plurality of religious beliefs, as well as a growing immigrant population, institutions that were meant to protect the individual can suddenly become hurtful and conflictual. Paying close attention to signs of conflict can then be helpful. Some early symptoms of conflict are subtle. Conflict usually starts with an erosion of trust between the parties involved and manifests through communication break downs, seeking someone to blame, and looking for scapegoats. Many signs of existing conflict include:

- demographic changes;
- population displacement;
- rising unemployment rates;
- economic shocks or financial crises;
- destruction or desecration of religious sites;

15. Porter, *Spirit and Art of Conflict Transformation*, 11.

- discrimination or legislation favoring one group over another;
- government clamp-downs;
- destabilizing an election;
- a rise in intolerance and prejudice; and
- an increase in numbers of demonstrations or rallies.[16]

These signs point to underlying conditions that need to be addressed before they escalate into a full-blown conflict.

Transformation

Conflict is inevitable in society; therefore, it is necessary to explore viable methods of conflict transformation. Humans create conflicts and only they can resolve them. Conflict transformation requires that both sides involved in a conflict not only attempt to resolve matters, but also eventually get involved in the transformation process, what Lederach calls the "journey towards reconciliation."[17] Conflict transformation necessitates continuous interaction between the groups as a way of transforming hostile relationships and simultaneously creating interaction among people at all levels.

Semiotic Signs of Building Peace

Throughout history, the development of the major monotheistic religions—Judaism, Islam, and Christianity—shows that humans themselves developed religious ideas into institutions with patterns of doctrines that saw each system as separate and unique. In *The Meaning and End of Religion*, Wilfred Cantwell Smith described how the institutions of religion developed as a clear and bounded historical phenomena. Smith explained that the adherents to these three religions "together make up well over half of the world's population."[18] He further shows that "without peace and conflict

---

16. Lederach, *Journey Toward Reconciliation*, 14.
17. Lederach, *Journey Toward Reconciliation*, 11.
18. Smith, *Meaning and End of Religion*, 9.

transformation between these religious communities, there can be no meaningful peace and conflict transformation in the world."[19] Therefore, "the future of the world depends on a common, semiotic understanding of nonviolence and conflict transformation."[20]

The "basis for this semiotic understanding already exists. It is part of the very foundational principles of these faiths: love of the divine and love of the neighbor. These principles are found over and over again in the sacred texts of Islam."[21] In Christianity and Judaism, "the necessity of love for this one God and the necessity of love of the neighbor is thus the common ground between these faiths."[22] Where love exists, violence and conflict tend to disintegrate.

Each of these religions has different symbolic systems that communicate meaning. Religious symbols are never completely arbitrary, suggesting they are a symbolic signifier that sees bonds. Semantically speaking, symbols are typically things with important historical and cultural meanings, such as the "cross for Christians, the star of David for the Jews, or the star and crescent for Muslims."[23]

All these symbols have one thing in common—they are tied to the history of each religion and play an important role in the culture of each faith tradition, as well as society in general. The role of religion in conflict transformation is vital if peace is to be attained. It is certainly true that religion and religious beliefs have powerful ingredients in many conflicts that are being underestimated. Religious grounds and ideologies have often helped people to reduce conflict, be it in Europe, Africa, the Middle East, or Asia. Examples of religion as an ingredient in conflict are not limited to interaction between Christians and Muslims, but can be found with other religions as well.[24]

Most religious communities share a language of faith. In that sense, they become members of a linguistic community. To belong

---

19. Smith, *Meaning and End of Religion*, 10.
20. Smith, *Meaning and End of Religion*, 11.
21. Rodrigues and Harding, *Introduction to the Study of Religion*, 11.
22. Rodrigues and Harding, *Introduction to the Study of Religion*, 15.
23. Rodrigues and Harding, *Introduction to the Study of Religion*, 12.
24. Nazir-Ali, *Conviction and Conflict*, 33.

to a religious community, people must learn and have a share in the community's faith language. The Abrahamic faiths trace their origin to Abraham and proclaim the doctrine of peacemaking as one of the driving forces of these religions. However, these faiths have different attachments to a sign, referent, and signifier to Abraham, and to the sign of their religious symbols. They each speak of Abraham in different terms and contexts and assign differing meanings to his story and their place in it. This lack of common reference becomes a problem because theological semiotics is not only the study of signs by which God's existence may be revealed to us, but also the study of signifying practice by which theological ideas may be expressed.

The absence of a semiotic approach among the Abrahamic faiths then becomes a challenge. However, the symbol of a dove to signify peace seems to be one that is understood and accepted across these faiths. This truth suggests that emphasis should be placed on the dove as a signifier for peace and conflict transformation. The cross, the crescent moon, and the star of David are signs that are subjective with these religions. On the other hand, I wonder: If these three signs are merged, would it not point to their Abrahamic origins? In asking this question, I am using Peirce's concept of the symbol, that is, "a symbol as a sign which refers to the object that it denotes by virtue of a law, usually an association of general ideas."[25] Simply said, the idea of combining these religious symbols is to establish the fact that the Abrahamic faiths are peace-loving and conflict-transforming religions.

When semiotics are not missed

We have thus far learned from semiotics that "we live in a world of signs, and we have no way of understanding anything except through signs."[26] These signs help us make sense of things, as they make us aware of the world around us. So, when we do not use semiotics, we begin to assign different meanings to objects. This

---

25. Chandler, *Semiotics*, 39.

26. Smith-Laing, *Analysis of Jacques Derrida's Structure, Sign, and Play*, 242.

tendency has the potential to cause conflict. Also, when semiotics is not used, the ability to do a satisfactory conflict transformation is limited.

1. Conflict mediation can be seen as the process in which conflicting parties discuss their concern, exploring existing possibilities to arrive at a mutually satisfactory solution to the conflict. However, little effort is given to the addressing of the underlying conditions leading up to the conflict. This process may be problematic in a victim and offender situation because conflict mediation tends to focus on the outcome rather than long-term transformation of the cause of the conflict.
2. Conflict resolution can simply be understood as the way in which conflicting parties find a peaceful solution to a disagreement. So, when a disagreement arises, conflict resolution by way of mediation is often explored to find solutions to the problem and end it. The focus is content-centered, and the purpose is to "achieve an agreement and solution to the presenting problem."[27]
3. Conflict transformation focuses on developing a new set of lenses for the immediate situation as well as the underlying pattern and context, in order to develop a conceptual framework that would lead to transformation. Conflict transformation therefore "seeks to create a framework to address the content, in this case the conflict, context, and structure for future and better relationships."[28]
    a. Lederach argued that a development of a conflict framework is needed if a conflict is to be transformed. This framework is contained in three elements:
        1. "it sees conflict as a long-term process, which occurs in the context of an ongoing relationship"[29];
        2. the framework has to employ an adequate descriptive language (common semantic); and

---

27. Derrida, "Structure, Sign, and Play," 242.
28. Lederach, *Preparing for Peace*, 22.
29. Lederach, *Preparing for Peace*, 24.

3. the framework should also incorporate an appreciation for the people as they seek to understand the peacemaking process.[30]

b. King's nonviolent approach. When Martin Luther King, Jr. confronted racism in the white church in the South, he called on those churches not to become more secular, but more Christian. King knew that the answer to racism and violence was not less Christianity but a deeper and truer Christianity. King gained his inspiration from the One who said that those who follow him must turn the other cheek, love their enemies, and pray for those who persecute them (Matt 5:38). King's leadership of the civil rights struggle remains an example of love triumphing over hate, costly and courageous resistance of evil, and religiously inspired social action that made the kind of difference everyone can appreciate.[31]

These ideals are King's expressions of his interpretation and application of the teachings of Jesus from the "Sermon on the Mount found in the gospel of Matthew."[32]

QUESTIONS OF REFLECTION

- What are some of the costs of pursuing conflict transformation for you and your group?
- What are some of the costs of not pursing transformation?
- How do you see God at work in the art of practicing what you preach in your separate congregations?

30. Lederach, *Toward Reconciliation*, 13. Lederach's description of reconciliation expressed the key to understanding conflict transformation is embedded in language. A common language then becomes the frame of reference that participants can learn to juxtapose personal transformation with systemic transformation. I would say, however, that transformation that is guided and shaped by a religious understanding seems to have a lasting impact on society as a whole.

31. King Jr., *Stride Toward Freedom*, 36.

32. King Jr., *Stride Toward Freedom*, 36.

Postscript

"Love is the only force capable of transforming an enemy into a friend."[1]

ANALYSIS: THE CHANGES FACED BY RELIGIONS

We stand at a juncture of different perspectives in religious beliefs, practices, and application when it comes to peace and conflict transformation and the awareness that every generation is called to this work. Each generation must address the challenges of its time.

One of the great challenges for this generation is the rise in violence and conflict, especially when such conflict is influenced by religious convictions. The 9/11 attacks brought to light what had been simmering for a long time—a perspective of hopelessness that came about as a result of religious disillusionment.

"Where do we go from here? What contribution can religion make, if any, to this state of affairs? Do the Abrahamic faiths need to experience being in relationship—not out of relationship with each other?"[2] The world as we see it today is experiencing a collapse of physical, political, and religious boundaries. These religions need to experience and share their commonality so that when it comes to peace and conflict transformation their peace heritages are clearly communicated to their adherents.

1. King Jr., *Strength to Love*, 122.
2. Norenzayan, "Does Religion Make People Moral?," 366.

Shared experience is necessary if religiously motivated terrorism is to be confronted and suffering alleviated. Finding a counterpoint to lighten the suffering of those who turn to divisive religious belief systems is imperative. A united Christian, Muslim, and Jewish response will be important if peace and conflict transformation are to take hold and bring transformation.

The Abrahamic faiths are therefore called to demonstrate a sense of oneness with one another, displayed through:

- compassionate living that draws from their religious traditions of respect and care for the community life. If adherents can rediscover and take hold of that heritage, they can build multireligious communities that participate in conflict transformation activities together.
- a willingness to critique some of the challenging texts in their Scriptures, and to acknowledge tendencies within these religion traditions that lead to a sense of pride and arrogance and a misbelief about having no need for the other. In addressing these issues, leaders and adherents seek to refresh an understanding that embraces the other religions in a spirit of mutuality and partnership.
- simple living. Instead of seeking to dominate one another, develop a spirit of mutual respect, seeking the humility to recognize and accept that other Abrahamic families have special emphases that your tradition does not have, and to accept the others' uniqueness in the spirit of partnership.
- welcoming religious diversity. Such practices will promote peace that results in conflict transformation.

The process of putting these steps into practice may be derived from some common responses to shared human suffering by seeking a common semiotic understanding of conflict and conflict transformation. These terms may need to be developed into an established framework within which a specific semiotic understanding will be carried out.

Bibliography

Abu-Nimer, Mohammed. "Conflict Resolution in an Islamic Context: Some Conceptual Questions." *Peace & Change* 21.1 (1996) 22–40.
———. *Nonviolence and Peace Building in Islam: Theory and Practice.* Gainesville, FL: University Press of Florida Press, 2003.
Alalwani, Taha Jabir. *The Ethics of Disagreement in Islam.* Herndon, VA: International Institute of Islamic Thought, 2011.
Albera, Dionigi, and Maria Couroucli, eds. *Sharing Sacred Spaces in the Mediterranean: Christians, Muslims, and Jews at Shrines and Sanctuaries.* Bloomington: Indiana University Press, 2012.
Ali B, Ali-Dinar, Page editor, African Studies Center. MLK, Letter from Birmingham Jail, accessed January 12, 2021. https://www.africa.upenn.edu/Articles_Gen/Letter_Birmingham.html
Amstutz, Mark R. "Is Reconciliation Possible After Genocide? The Case of Rwanda." *Journal of Church and State* (2006) 541–65.
Angelou, Maya. *Maya Angelou.* New York: Sterling, 2007.
Appleby, R. Scott. *The Ambivalence of the Sacred: Religion, Violence, and Reconciliation.* Lanham, MD: Rowman & Littlefield, 2000.
Armster, Michelle, and Lorraine Stutzman Amstutz. *Conflict Transformation and Restorative Justice Manual.* Akron, PA: Mennonite Conciliation Service, 2008.
Armstrong, Karen. *A History of God: The 4000-Year Quest of Judaism, Christianity and Islam.* New York: Ballentine, 1993.
Augsburger, David. *Conflict Mediation across Cultures: Pathways and Patterns.* Louisville: Westminster/John Knox Press, 1992.
Avruch, Kevin. *Culture and Conflict Resolution.* Washington, DC: United States Institute of Peace Press, 1998
Baddon, Lesley, et al. *People's Capitalism?: A Critical Analysis of Profit-Sharing and Employee Share Ownership.* Milton Park, UK: Taylor & Francis, 2017.
Baldwin, Elaine. *Introducing Cultural Studies.* London: Pearson Education, 2004.

BIBLIOGRAPHY

Bateson, Gregory, and Mary Catherine Bateson. *Angels Fear: Towards an Epistemology of the Sacred*. New York: Bantam, 1987.

Bauman, Zygmunt. *Community: Seeking Safety in an Insecure World*. Hoboken, NJ: Wiley & Sons, 2013.

Bell, Daniel M. *Just War as Christian Discipleship*. Eugene, OR: Wipf and Stock, 2005.

Bercovitch, Jacob. "International Mediation and Dispute Settlement: Evaluating the Conditions for Successful Mediation." *Negotiation Journal* 7.1 (1991) 17–30.

Bergen, Peter L. "September 11 Attacks." *Encyclopaedia Britannica*, revised April 5, 2017, https://www.britannica.com/event/September-11-attacks.

Berger, Arthur A. *Seeing Is Believing: An Introduction to Visual Communication*. Houston: Mayfield, 1989.

———. *Signs in Contemporary Culture: An Introduction to Semiotics*. Salem, WI: Sheffield, 1998.

Berndt, Hagen. *Non-violence in the World Religions: Vision and Reality*. London: SCM, 2000.

Biggar, Nigel. *Burying the Past: Making Peace and Doing Justice after Civil Conflict*. Washington, DC: Georgetown University Press, 2003.

Blakey, Michael L., et al. *African Roots/American Cultures: Africa in the Creation of the Americas*. Lanham, MD: Rowman & Littlefield, 2001.

Block, Peter. *The Answer to How Is Yes: Acting on What Matters*. San Francisco: Berrett-Koehler, 2002.

Blumenthal, Ralph. "Fire in the Bronx; 87 Die in Blaze at Illegal Club; Police Arrest Ejected Patron; Worst New York Fire Since 1911." *The New York Times*, March 26, 1990. https://www.nytimes.com/1990/03/26/nyregion/fire-bronx-87-die-blaze-illegal-club-police-arrest-ejected-patron-worst-new-york.html.

Boege, Volker. "Traditional Approaches to Conflict Transformation: Potentials and Limits." http://edoc.vifapol.de/opus/volltexte/2011/2565/pdf/boege_handbook.pdf.

Bonhoeffer, Dietrich. *The Cost of Discipleship*. New York: Simon and Schuster, 2012.

Botes, Johannes. "Conflict Transformation: A Debate over Semantics or a Crucial Shift in the Theory and Practice of Peace and Conflict Studies?" *International Journal of Peace Studies* (2003) 1–27.

Bouckaert, Peter N. "The Negotiated Revolution: South Africa's Transition to a Multiracial Democracy." *Stanford Journal of International Law* 33 (1997) 375–450.

Bowman, Carl F. *Brethren Society: The Cultural Transformation of a "Peculiar People."* Baltimore: Johns Hopkins University Press, 1995.

Brewer, John D., et al. "Religion and Peacemaking: A Conceptualization." *Sociology* 44.6 (2010) 1019–37.

Brogden, Mike, and Preeti Nijhar. *Community Policing National and International Approaches*. Abingdon, UK: Routledge, 2013.

BIBLIOGRAPHY

Brueggemann, Walter. *Isaiah: 1–39.* Vol. 1. 2 vols. Louisville: Westminster John Knox Press, 1998.

Burke, Kenneth. *The Rhetoric of Religion: Studies in Logology.* Berkeley: University of California Press, 1970.

Burton, John. *Conflict Resolution and Prevention.* New York: St. Martin's, 1990.

Carey, Benedict. *How We Learn: The Surprising Truth About When, Where and Why It Happens.* New York: Random House, 2015.

Chandler, Daniel. *Semiotics: The Basics.* New York: Routledge, 2017.

Charles, J. Daryl and Timothy J. Demy. *War, Peace, and Christianity: Questions and Answers from a Just-War Perspective.* Wheaton, IL: Crossway, 2010.

Childers, R. C. "Art. VII—Khuddaka Páṭha, a Páli Text, with a Translation and Notes." *Journal of the Royal Asiatic Society* 4.2 (January 1870) 309–39. https://doi.org/10.1017/S0035869X00016002.

Chittister, Joan, et al. *The Tent of Abraham: Stories of Hope and Peace for Jews, Christians, and Muslims.* Boston: Beacon, 2007.

Chödrön, Pema, and Sandy Boucher. *Practicing Peace in Times of War.* Boulder, CO: Shambhala, 2007.

Conner, Benjamin T. "Darrell L. Guder." *Princeton Theological Review* 18.1 (2015) 5–9.

Copeland-Carson, Jacqueline. *Creating Africa in America: Translocal Identity in an Emerging World City.* Philadelphia: University of Pennsylvania Press, 2012.

Corrington, Robert S. *A Semiotic Theory of Theology and Philosophy.* Cambridge: Cambridge University Press, 2000.

Curry, Corina. "People Who Care: It All Began 20 Years Ago." *Rockford Register Star*, February 24, 2009. www.rrstar.com/article/20090224/News/302249850.

Cyplick, Amy. "People Who Care v. Rockford School District: The Repercussions of Using Legal Means to Right Social Wrongs." Master's thesis, Southern Illinois University Carbondale, 2013. http://opensiuc.lib.siu.edu/cgi/viewcontent.cgi?article=1444&context=gs_rp.

Dallmayr, Fred R., ed. *Border Crossings: Toward a Comparative Political Theory.* New York: Lexington, 2000.

Dear, John. *The God of Peace: Toward a Theology of Nonviolence.* Eugene, OR: Wipf and Stock, 2005.

———. *Seeds of Nonviolence.* Eugene, OR: Wipf and Stock, 2008.

Deely, John N. *Basics of Semiotics.* Bloomington: Indiana University Press, 1990.

Denning, Steve. "The Science of Storytelling," *Forbes*, March 9, 2012. https://www.forbes.com/sites/stevedenning/2012/03/09/the-science-of-storytelling/#4e3c1ad52d8a.

Déogratias, Fikiri. "Mercy in a Conflictual Society: An Inward Journey Toward Reconciliation." *Hekima Review* 54 (2016) 15–24.

De Saussure, Ferdinand, and Wade Baskin. *Course in General Linguistics [1916].* London: Duckworth, 2011.

Deutsch, Morton, et al., eds. *The Handbook of Conflict Resolution: Theory and Practice.* New York: Wiley & Sons, 2011.

Dirks, Jerald F. *The Abrahamic Faiths: Judaism, Christianity, and Islam: Similarities and Contrasts.* Beltsville, MD: Amana, 2004.

Douglass, Susan L., and Munir A. Shaikh. "Defining Islamic Education: Differentiation and Applications." *Current Issues in Comparative Education* 7.1 (December 2004) 5–18.

Downing, Crystal L. *Changing Signs of Truth: A Christian Introduction to the Semiotics of Communication.* Downers Grove, IL: InterVarsity, 2012.

Drucker, Susan J., and Robert S. Cathcart, eds. *American Heroes in a Media Age.* Cresskill, NJ: Hampton, 1994.

Eco, Umberto. *Semiotics and the Philosophy of Language.* Bloomington: Indiana University Press, 1986.

———. *A Theory of Semiotics.* Bloomington: Indiana University Press, 1976.

Edwards, Harry T. "Alternative Dispute Resolution: Panacea or Anathema?" *Harvard Law Review* 99.3 (1986) 668–84.

Edwards, Brent Hayes. "The Uses of 'Diaspora.'" In *African Diasporas in the New and Old Worlds: Consciousness and Imagination,* edited by Genevieve Fabre and Klaus Benesch, 161–81. New York: Rodopi, 2004.

Eller, Jack David. *From Culture to Ethnicity to Conflict: An Anthropological Perspective on International Ethnic Conflict.* Ann Arbor: University of Michigan Press, 1999.

Emerick, Yahiya. *The Life and Work of Muhammad.* London: Penguin, 2002.

Enns, Fernando, et al. *Seeking Cultures of Peace: A Peace Church Conversation.* Telford, PA: Cascadia House, 2004.

Falk, Richard. "False Universalism and the Geopolitics of Exclusion: The Case of Islam." *Third World Quarterly* 18.1 (1997) 7–23.

Finn, Daniel K. *The Moral Ecology of Markets: Assessing Claims about Markets and Justice.* Cambridge, UK: Cambridge University Press, 2006.

Fisher, Roger, et al. *Getting to Yes: Negotiating Agreement without Giving in.* 2nd ed. New York: Penguin, 1991.

Fisk, Shannon. "The Importance of Full Court Involvement: A Case Study of the Rockford, IL School Desegregation Efforts." https://www.clearinghouse.net/chDocs/resources/caseStudy_ShannonFisk_1221018359.pdf.

Flicker, Barbara. *Justice and School Systems: The Role of the Courts in Education Litigation.* Philadelphia: Temple University Press, 2011.

Fry, Douglas P. "Conflict Management in Cross-cultural Perspective." *Natural Conflict Resolution* (2000) 334–51.

Funk, Nathan C., and Abdul Aziz Said. *Islam and Peacemaking in the Middle East.* Boulder, CO: Rienner, 2009.

Gabel, Peter. "The Spiritual Dimension of Social Justice." *Journal of Legal Education.* 673 (2013) 673–88.

Galtung, Johan. "Conflict Life Cycles in Occident and Orient." In *Cultural Variation in Conflict Resolution: Alternatives to Violence,* edited by Douglas P. Fry and Kai Bjorkqvist, 16–24. Mahwah, NJ: Erlbaum Associates, 1997.

———. "Violence, Peace, and Peace Research." *Journal of Peace Research* 6.3 (1969) 167–91.

Gandhi, Mahatma. *All Men Are Brothers: Autobiographical Reflections*. London: Black, 1980.

Geary, James. *I Is an Other: The Secret Life of Metaphor and How It Shapes the Way We See the World*. New York: Harper Collins, 2011.

Gehm, John R. "Victim-Offender Mediation Programs: An Exploration of Practice and Theoretical Frameworks." *Western Criminology Review* 1.1 (1998) 1–30.

Gellman, Mneesha, and Mandi Vuinovich. "From Sulha to Salaam: Connecting Local Knowledge with International Negotiations for Lasting Peace in Palestine/Israel." *Conflict Resolution Quarterly* 26.2 (2008) 127–48.

Gibson, James L. "Overcoming Apartheid: Can Truth Reconcile a Divided Nation?" *The Annals of the American Academy of Political and Social Science* 603.1 (2006) 82–110.

Gopin, Marc. "Religion, Violence, and Conflict Resolution." *Peace & Change* 22 (1997) 1–31.

Greig, Pete. *Dirty Glory: Go Where Your Best Prayers Take You*. Vol. 2. 2 vols. Colorado Springs, CO: NavPress, 2016.

Grim, Brian J. "Religious Freedom: Good for What Ails Us?" *The Review of Faith & International Affairs* 6.2 (2008) 3–7.

Grim, Brian J., and Roger Finke. *The Price of Freedom Denied: Religious Persecution and Conflict in the Twenty-First Century*. Boston: Cambridge University Press, 2010.

Griswold, Eliza. *The Tenth Parallel: Dispatches from the Fault Line Between Christianity and Islam*. New York: Farrar, Straus and Giroux, 2010.

Gushee, David P., ed. *Evangelical Peacemakers: Gospel Engagement in a War-Torn World*. Eugene, OR: Wipf and Stock, 2013.

Halverson, Jeffry R. *Searching for a King: Muslim Nonviolence and the Future of Islam*. 1st ed. Washington, DC: Potomac, 2012.

Hartshorn, Leo. "A Theo-Politics of Reconciliation." *A Different Drummer* (blog), January 3, 2009. http://leohartshorn.blogspot.com/2008/01/theo-politics-of-reconciliation.html.

Hastings, Tom H. *The Lessons of Nonviolence: Theory and Practice in a World of Conflict*. Jefferson, NC: McFarland, 2006.

Haught, John F. *Resting on the Future: Catholic Theology for an Unfinished Universe*. New York: Bloomsbury USA, 2015.

Hehir, J. Bryan, et al. *Liberty and Power: A Dialogue on Religion and U.S. Foreign Policy in an Unjust World*. Washington, DC: Brookings Institution Press, 2004.

Hendrie, Caroline. "Settlement Ends St. Louis School Desegregation Case." *Education Week*, March 24, 1999. http://www.edweek.org/ew/vol-18/2810uis.hl8.

Hick, John, and Brian Hebblethwaite. *Christianity and Other Religions: Selected Readings*. London: Oneworld, 2014.

Hodge, Robert, et al. *Social Semiotics*. Ithaca, NY: Cornell University Press, 1988.

Holz, Joanne L. "Biblical Hospitality: An Environment for Leader Development. 2016. Dissertation, accessed January 13, 2021. https://digitalcommons.georgefox.edu/cgi/viewcontent.cgi?article=1132&context=dmin

Hollinger, David A. *Postethnic America: Beyond Multiculturalism*. London: Hachette UK, 2006.

Huntington, Samuel P. *Who Are We? The Challenges to America's National Identity*. Delran, NJ: Simon and Schuster, 2004.

Hutchison, Peggy, and Harmon Wray. "What Is Restorative Justice?" *New World Outlook* (1999) 1–6.

Idliby, Ranya, et al. *The Faith Club: A Muslim, a Christian, a Jew—Three Women Search for Understanding*. Delran, NJ: Simon & Schuster, 2007.

Bernard Lafayette, Jr. and David Jensen, The Community Leader's Workbook; The Kingian Nonviolence Conflict Reconciliation Program. Institute for Human Rights and Responsibilities. IHRR Publications l 73 Walnut Street N. Galena, Ohio 2017.

Irani, George E. and Nathan C. Funk. "Rituals of Reconciliation: Arab Islamic Perspectives." *Arab Studies Quarterly* 20.4 (1998) 53–73.

Iversen, Katja. "Applying a Gender Lens to COVID-19 Response and Recovery." *Medium*, May 5, 2020. https://medium.com/@Katja_Iversen/applying-a-gender-lens-to-covid-19-response-and-recovery-2fe19255746f.

Jackson, Robert. *Classical and Modern Thought on International Relations: From Anarchy to Cosmopolis*. New York: Palgrave Macmillan, 2005.

Johnston, Douglas, and Cynthia Sampson, eds. *Religion: The Missing Dimension of Statecraft*. New York: Oxford University Press, 1994.

Johnstone, Gerry. *Restorative Justice: Ideas, Values, Debates*. Abingdon, UK: Routledge, 2013.

John Horgan, Ancient History Encyclopedia, Antonine Plague, Published May 2, 2019, accessed January 20, 2021 https://www.ancient.eu/Antonine_Plague/

Jones, L. Gregory. "Practicing Peacemaking." http://www.catalystresources.org/practicing-peacemaking/

Jordan, Tim. *Activism! Direct Action, Hacktivism and the Future of Society*. London: Reaktion, 2002.

Karas, Tania. "A Tale of Two Sanctuary Churches: Congregants in Ohio and the Netherlands Find Instant Connection." *The World*, January 21, 2019. https://www.pri.org/stories/2019-01-21/tale-two-sanctuary-churches-congregants-ohio-and-netherlands-find-instant

Kateregga, Badru D., and David W. Shenk. *A Muslim and a Christian in Dialogue*. Harrisonburg, VA: Herald, 2011.

Katongole, Emmanuel. "Greeting Beyond Racial Reconciliation." In *The Blackwell Companion to Christian Ethics*, 1st ed., edited by Stanley Hauerwas and Samuel Wells, 70–83. Chichester: Wiley-Blackwell, 2006.

Katongole, Emmanuel, and Chris Rice. *Reconciling All Things: A Christian Vision for Justice, Peace, and Healing*. Downers Grove, IL: InterVarsity, 2009.
Kayaoglu, Turan. "Preachers of Dialogue: International Relations and Interfaith Theology." *And Peacebuilding* (2007) 147–52.
Kemp, Karen Margaret. "Transforming Congregational Conflict: An Integrated Framework for Understanding and Addressing Conflict in Christian Faith Communities." Master's thesis University of Wellington, 2010. http://hdl.handle.net/10063/1524.
Kim, Heon. *A Just World: Multi-Disciplinary Perspectives on Social Justice*. New York: Cambridge Scholars, 2014.
King, Martin Luther, Jr. "*America's Chief Moral Dilemma.*" 1967 audio sermon. *American Archive of Public Broadcasting.* 1:12:11. https://americanarchive.org/catalog/cpb-aacip_28-fn1opox51h
———. "I've Been to the Mountaintop." https://www.britannica.com/event/assassination-of-Martin-Luther-King-Jr/The-Mountaintop-Speech
———. "Letter from a Birmingham Jail." http://okra.stanford.edu/transcription/document_images/undecided/630416-019.pdf.
———. "Nobel Lecture." https://www.nobelprize.org/prizes/peace/1964/king/lecture/
———. *Radical King*. King Legacy Vol. 11. 11 vols. Boston: Beacon, 2015.
———. *Strength to Love*. New York: Harper & Row, 1963.
———. *Stride Toward Freedom: The Montgomery Story*. Edited by Clayborne Carson. Boston: Beacon, 2010.
———. I've Been to the Mountaintop 1968, accessed January 12,2021. https://www.britannica.com/event/assassination-of-Martin-Luther-King-Jr/The-Mountaintop-Speech
———. The Radical King. Edited by Cornel West. The King Legacy Series, Vol.11 Beacon Press, 2015.
Konadu-Agyemang, Kwadwo, and Baffour K. Takyi. "An Overview of African Immigration to US and Canada." In *The New African Diaspora in North America: Trends, Community Building, and Adaptation*, edited by Kwado Konadu-Agyemang et al, 1–27. Lanham, MD: Rowman & Littlefield, 2006.
Kurlansky, Mark. *Nonviolence: The History of a Dangerous Idea*. New York: Modern Library, 2009.
LaFayette, Bernard, and David C. Jehnsen. *The Leader's Manual: A Structured Guide and Introduction to Kingian Nonviolence: The Philosophy and Methodology*. Galena, IL: Institute for Human Rights and Responsibilities, 1995.
Lak, Martijn. "A Political History of the World: Three Thousand Years of War and Peace by Jonathan Holslag." *Journal of World History* 30.4 (2019) 642–45.
Langermann, Y. Tzvi, ed. *Monotheism & Ethics: Historical and Contemporary Intersections Among Judaism, Christianity and Islam*. Vol. 2. 11 vols. Leiden: Brill, 2011.

BIBLIOGRAPHY

Lansing, Paul, and Julie C. King. "South Africa's Truth and Reconciliation Commission: The Conflict Between Individual Justice and National Healing in the Post-Apartheid Age." *Arizona Journal of International and Comparative Law* 15 (1998) 753–870.

Larson, Colleen L., and Khaula Murtadha. "Leadership for Social Justice." *Yearbook of the National Society for the Study of Education* 101.1 (2002) 134–61.

Lartey, Jamiles. "Predatory Police: The High Price of Driving While Black in Missouri." *The Guardian*, July 5, 2018. https://www.theguardian.com/us-news/2018/jul/05/missouri-driving-while-black-st-louis

Laue, James H. "Contributions of the Emerging Field of Conflict Resolution." In *Approaches to Peace: An Intellectual Map*, edited by W. Scott Thompson and Kenneth M. Jensen, 299–332. Washington, DC: United States Institute of Peace Press, 1988.

Lederach, John Paul. *The Journey Toward Reconciliation*. Scottdale, PA: Herald, 1999.

———. *The Little Book of Conflict Transformation: Clear Articulation of the Guiding Principles by a Pioneer in the Field*. Intercourse, PA: Good, 2003.

———. "The Mediator's Cultural Assumptions." In *Mediation and Facilitation Training Manual: Foundations and Skills for Constructive Conflict Transformation*, 3rd ed., edited by Jim Stutzman and Carolyn Schrock-Shenk, 80–82. Akron, PA: Mennonite Conciliation Service, 1995.

———. *The Moral Imagination: The Art and Soul of Building Peace*. New York: Oxford University Press, 2005.

———. *Preparing for Peace: Conflict Transformation Across Cultures*. Ithaca, NY: Syracuse University Press, 1996.

Leithart, Peter J. *Traces of the Trinity: Signs of God in Creation and Human Experience*. Grand Rapids: Brazos, 2015.

Leonhardt, David. "Dave Rothenberg, Whose Father Set Him on Fire in 1983, Dies at 42." *The New York Times*, August 17, 2018. https://www.nytimes.com/2018/08/17/obituaries/dave-rothenberg-whose-father-set-him-on-fire-in-1983-dies-at-42.html.

Levine, Amy-Jill, and Marc Z. Brettler. *The Jewish Annotated New Testament*. Oxford: Oxford University Press, 2011.

Lichtblau, Eric. "U.S. Hate Crimes Surge 6%, Fueled by Attacks on Muslims." *New York Times*, November 15, 2016. https://www.nytimes.com/2016/11/15/us/politics/fbi-hate-crimes-muslims.html?mcubz=1.

Lippy, Charles H. *Pluralism Comes of Age: American Religious Culture in the Twentieth Century*. Armonk, NY: Sharpe, 2000.

Lydersen, Kari. "Shooting by Police Ignites Racial Tensions in Illinois Town." *Washington Post*, October 4, 2009. http://www.washingtonpost.com/wp-dyn/content/article/2009/10/03/AR2009100302144.html.

Mackenzie, Don, et al. *Getting to the Heart of Interfaith*. Woodstock, VT: Skylight Paths, 2010.

MacNair, Rachel M. *Religions and Nonviolence: The Rise of Effective Advocacy for Peace*. Santa Barbara, CA: ABC-CLIO, 2015.
Mann, Gurinder Singh, et al. *Buddhists, Hindus and Sikhs in America: A Short History*. Oxford: Oxford University Press, 2007.
Marshall, Tony F. *Restorative Justice: An Overview*. London: Home Office Research Development and Statistics Directorate, 1999.
Martin, David. *The Breaking of the Image: A Sociology of Christian Theory and Practice*. Vancouver: Regent College Press, 2006
Matyók, Thomas, et al., eds. *Peace on Earth: The Role of Religion in Peace and Conflict Studies*, Lanham, MD: Lexington, 2014.
Mazrui, Ali. "Islamic and Western Values." *Foreign Affairs* 76.5 (September-October 1997) 118–32.
McCrummen, Stephanie. "A Sanctuary of One." *The Washington Post*, March 31, 2018. https://www.washingtonpost.com/news/national/wp/2018/03/31/feature/after-30-years-in-america-she-was-about-to-be-deported-then-a-tiny-colorado-church-offered-her-sanctuary/
McCutcheon, Richard, et al. *Voices of Harmony and Dissent: How Peacebuilders Are Transforming Their Worlds*. Winnipeg, MB: Canadian Mennonite University Press, 2015.
McDaniel, Jay Byrd. *Gandhi's Hope: Learning from Other Religions as a Path to Peace*. Maryknoll, NY: Orbis, 2005.
McNeil, Brenda Salter. *Roadmap to Reconciliation: Moving Communities into Unity, Wholeness and Justice*. Downers Grove, IL: InterVarsity, 2016.
Mearsheimer, John J. and Stephen M. Walt. *The Israel Lobby and U.S. Foreign Policy*. New York: Macmillan, 2007.
Menkel-Meadow, Carrie J., and Lela Porter-Love. *Mediation: Practice, Policy, and Ethics*. Alphen aan den Rijn, NL: Wolters Kluwer Law & Business Group, 2014.
Meyer, Erin. *The Culture Map: Breaking Through the Invisible Boundaries of Global Business*. New York: Public Affairs, 2014.
Miller, Allen O., ed. *Reconciliation in Today's World: Six Study Papers*. Grand Rapids: Eerdmans, 1969.
Mitchell, Christopher. "Beyond Resolution: What Does Conflict Transformation Actually Transform?" *Peace and Conflict Studies* 9.1 (2002) 1–23.
Moeschberger, Scott L., and Rebekah A. Phillips DeZalia. *Symbols that Bind, Symbols that Divide*. Basel: Springer Switzerland, 2014.
Moravcsik, Andrew. "Negotiating the Single European Act: National Interests and Conventional Statecraft in the European Community." *International Organization* 45.1 (1991) 19–56.
Morrison, John M. "Reconciliation in Today's World." In *Six Study Papers*, edited by AO Miller, 379–80. Grand Rapids: Eerdmans, 1970.
Moses, Rafael. "The Leader and the Led: A Dyadic Relationship." *The Psychodynamics of International Relationships* 1 (1990) 205–17.

BIBLIOGRAPHY

Mosher, Lucinda, and David Marshall, eds. *Sin, Forgiveness, and Reconciliation: Christian and Muslim Perspectives*. Washington, DC: Georgetown University Press, 2016.

Mother Teresa. *In the Heart of the World: Thoughts, Stories & Prayers*. Novato, CA: New World Library, 2010.

Myers, Joseph R. *The Search to Belong: Rethinking Intimacy, Community, and Small Groups*. Grand Rapids: Zondervan, 2003.

Nagler, Michael N. *The Search for a Nonviolent Future: A Promise of Peace for Ourselves, Our Families, and Our World*. Novato, CA: New World Library, 2010.

Nazir-Ali, Michael. *Conviction and Conflict: Islam, Christianity and World Order*. London: Black, 2006.

Newkirk, Vann R., II. "The Coronavirus's Unique Threat to the South." *The Atlantic*, April 2, 2020. https://www.theatlantic.com/politics/archive/2020/04/coronavirus-unique-threat-south-young-people/609241/.

Nodia, Georgi O. "Nationalism and Democracy." *Journal of Democracy* 3.4 (1992) 3–22.

Norenzayan, Ara. "Does Religion Make People Moral?" *Behaviour* 151.2–3 (2014) 365–84.

Pal, Amitabh. *Islam Means Peace: Understanding the Muslim Principle of Nonviolence Today*. Santa Barbara, CA: Praeger, 2011

Porter, Thomas W. *The Spirit and Art of Conflict Transformation: Creating a Culture of JustPeace*. Nashville: Upper Room, 2010.

Quinn, Robert E. *Change the World: How Ordinary People Can Accomplish Extraordinary Things*. San Francisco: Jossey-Bass, 2000.

Rausch, David A., and Carl Herman Voss. *World Religion: Our Quest for Meaning*. Patterson, NJ: Trinity, 1993.

Regan, Michael P. "Wall Street Seeks the Right Metaphor for the Virus Meltdown." *Bloomberg Businessweek*, February 26, 2020. https://www.bloomberg.com/news/articles/2020-02-26/wall-street-seeks-the-right-metaphor-for-the-virus-meltdown.

Reiss, Hans, ed. *Kant: Political Writings*. New York: Cambridge University Press, 1991.

Ricard, Matthieu. *Altruism: The Power of Compassion to Change Yourself and the World*. Boston: Little, Brown, 2015.

Ritterman, Jeff. "The Beloved Community: Martin Luther King Jr.'s Prescription for a Healthy Society." *Huffpost*, January 19, 2014. https://www.huffingtonpost.com/jeffrey-ritterman/the-beloved-community-dr-_b_4583249.html.

Roberson, Cliff, and Paul Harvey Wallace. *Family Violence: Legal, Medical, and Social Perspectives*. Abingdon, UK: Routledge, 2016.

Rodrigues, Hillary P., and John S. Harding. *Introduction to the Study of Religion*. Abingdon, UK: Routledge, 2008.

Root, Michael, and James J. Buckley, eds. *Christian Theology and Islam*. Vol. 2. 2 vols. Eugene, OR: Cascade, 2013.

Rosenberg, Gerald N. *The Hollow Hope: Can Courts Bring About Social Change?* Chicago, IL: University of Chicago Press, 2008.

Rosenberg, Marshall, and Deepak Chopra. *Nonviolent Communication: A Language of Life: Life-Changing Tools for Healthy Relationships*. Encinitas, CA: PuddleDancer, 2015.

Ross, Robert, et al., eds. *The Cambridge History of South Africa*, Vol. 2. 5 vols. New York: Cambridge University Press, 2011.

Ruskin, John. *The Letters of John Ruskin to Lord and Lady Mount-Temple*. Columbus: Ohio State University Press, 1964.

Ruskin, John, and Charles Eliot Norton. *The Correspondence of John Ruskin and Charles Eliot Norton*. Cambridge University Press, 1987.

Sablosky, Roy. "Does Religion Foster Generosity?" *The Social Science Journal* 51.4 (2014) 545–55.

Said, Abdul Aziz, et al. *Concepts of International Politics in Global Perspective*, 4th ed. Englewood Cliffs, NJ: Prentice Hall, 1995.

———. *Peace and Conflict Resolution in Islam: Precept and Practice*. Lanham, MD: University Press of America, 2001.

Salla, Michael. "Political Islam and the West: A New Cold War or Convergence?" *Third World Quarterly* 18.4 (1997) 729–42.

Saritoprak, Zeki, and Sidney Griffith. "Fethullah Gülen and the 'People of the Book': A Voice from Turkey for Interfaith Dialogue." *The Muslim World* 95.3 (2005) 329–40.

Satha Anand, Chaiwat. *The Nonviolent Crescent: Two Essays on Islam and Nonviolence*. IFOR Occasional Paper Series 3. Alkmaar, NL: International Fellowship of Reconciliation, 1996.

Schmidt-Leukel, Perry, ed. *War and Peace in World Religions: The Gerald Weisfeld Lectures 2003*. London: SCM, 2004.

Schumaker, Kathryn Anne. *Civil Rights and Uncivil Society: Education, Law, and the Struggle for Racial Equity in the Midwest, 1965–1980*. Chicago: University of Chicago Press, 2013.

Scimecca, Joseph A. "Conflict Resolution in the United States: The Emergence of a Profession." In *Conflict Resolution: Cross Cultural Perspectives*, edited by Kevin Avruch et al., 11–27. Westport, CT: Greenwood, 1991.

Scott, Alex. *Christian Semiotics and the Language of Faith*. New York: Universe, 2007.

Seekings, Jeremy, and Nicoli Nattrass. *Class, Race, and Inequality in South Africa*. New Haven: Yale University Press, 2008.

Segal, Alan F. *Paul the Convert: The Apostolate and Apostasy of Saul the Pharisee*. New Haven: Yale University Press, 1990.

Segler, Franklin M., and Randall Bradley. *Christian Worship: Its Theology and Practice*. Nashville: B&H, 2006.

Seidler, Victor J. "Religions, Hatreds, Peacemaking and Suffering." In *Can Faiths Make Peace? Holy Wars and the Resolution of Religious Conflicts*, edited by Philip Broadhead and Damien Keown, 27–47. New York: Tauris, 2007.

Bibliography

Sharma, Arvind, ed. *The World's Religions: A Contemporary Reader.* Minneapolis: Fortress, 2010.

Sharp, Gene, and Marina Finkelstein. *The Politics of Nonviolent Action.* Vol. 3. 5 vols. Boston: Sargent, 1973.

Shenk, David W. *Christian. Muslim. Friend: Twelve Paths to Real Relationship.* Harrisonburg, VA: Herald, 2014.

———. "The Gospel of Reconciliation Within the Wrath of Nations." *International Bulletin of Missionary Research* 32.1 (2008) 3–9.

Shilhav, Yosseph. "Principles for the Location of Synagogues: Symbolism and Functionalism in a Spatial Context." *The Professional Geographer* 35.3 (1983) 324–29.

Silverman, Kaja. *The Subject of Semiotics.* Oxford: Oxford University Press, 1984.

Skinner, Elliott Percival. *African Americans and US Policy Toward Africa, 1850–1924: In Defense of Black Nationality.* Washington DC: Howard University Press, 1992.

Smith, Huston, and Richard Marranca. *The World's Religions.* New York: HarperOne, 2009.

Smith, Wilfred Cantwell. *The Meaning and End of Religion.* Minneapolis: Fortress, 1963.

Smith-Christopher, Daniel L., ed. *Subverting Hatred: The Challenge of Nonviolence in Religious Traditions.* New York: Orbis, 2000.

Smith-Laing, Tim. *An Analysis of Jacques Derrida's Structure, Sign, and Play in the Discourse of the Human Sciences.* Milton Park, UK: Taylor & Francis, 2018.

Sprinkle, Preston. *Fight: A Christian Case for Non-Violence.* Elgin, IL: Cook, 2013.

Sri, Guru. *Granth Sahib.* Vol. 4. 34 vols. New Delhi: Allied, 1962.

Stassen, Glen Harold. *A Thicker Jesus: Incarnational Discipleship in a Secular Age.* Louisville: Westminster John Knox, 2012.

Stassen, Glen Harold, ed. *Just Peacemaking as the New Paradigm for the Ethics of Peace and War.* Boston: Pilgrim, 2008.

Stassen, Glen Harold, et al., eds. *Formation for Life: Just Peacemaking and Twenty-First-Century Discipleship.* Eugene, OR: Pickwick, 2013.

Stegemann, Ekkehard, and Wolfgang Stegemann. *Jesus Movement: A Social History of Its First Century.* London: Black, 1999.

Sweet, Leonard. *Aquachurch.* Loveland, CO: Group, 1999.

———. *The Bad Habits of Jesus: Showing Us the Way to Live Right in a World Gone Wrong.* Carol Stream, IL: Tyndale House, 2016.

———. *I Am a Follower: The Way, Truth, and Life of Following Jesus.* New York: Harper Collins, 2012.

———. *Me and We: God's New Social Gospel.* Nashville: Abingdon, 2014.

———. *Summoned to Lead.* Grand Rapids: Zondervan, 2004.

Tarnas, Richard. *The Passion of the Western Mind.* New York: Ballantine, 1991.

Tett, Gillian. *The Silo Effect: The Peril of Expertise and the Promise of Breaking Down Barriers.* New York: Simon & Schuster, 2015.

Thomas, Scott. *The Global Resurgence of Religion and the Transformation of International Relations: The Struggle for the Soul of the Twenty-First Century*. New York: Springer, 2005.

Tutu, Desmond. *No Future Without Forgiveness*. New York: Random House, 2012.

Tworek, Heidi. "The Creation of European News: News Agency Cooperation in Interwar Europe." *Journalism Studies* 14.5 (2013) 730–42.

Umbreit, Mark S., et al. "Restorative Justice Dialogue: A Multi-Dimensional, Evidence-Based Practice Theory." *Contemporary Justice Review* 10.1 (2007) 23–41.

Ury, William. *The Third Side: Why We Fight and How We Can Stop*. New York: Penguin, 2000.

Uvalić–Trumbić, Stamenka, and John Daniel. "Let a Thousand Flowers Bloom." A paper presented at the United Nations General Assembly UNESCO Global Forum, Paris, May 16–17, 2011.

Volf, Miroslav. "The Social Meaning of Reconciliation." *Occasional Papers on Religion in Eastern Europe* 18.3 (1998) 1–11.

Volney, Constantin-François. *The Ruins: Or, Meditation on the Revolutions of Empires: and the Law of Nature*. New York: Eckler, 1890.

Waardenburg, Jacques. "Christians, Muslims, Jews, and Their Religions." *Islam and Christian-Muslim Relations* 15.1 (2004) 13–33.

Walker, Sheila. *African Roots/American Cultures: Africa in the Creation of the Americas*. Lanham, MD: Rowman & Littlefield, 2001.

Wehr, Paul, and John Paul Lederach. "Mediating Conflict in Central America." *Journal of Peace Research* 38 (August 1993) 331–46.

Westbrook, David E. "Comparative Analysis of Conflict Resolution and Nonviolent Activism Leading to an Integrated Model for Peaceful Social Change." PhD diss., Portland State University, 2003.

Wiesel, Elie. *Against Silence: The Voice and Vision of Elie Wiesel*. Edited by Irving Abrahamson. Washington, DC: Holocaust Library, 1985.

Wink, Walter. *Jesus and Nonviolence: A Third Way*. Minneapolis: Fortress, 2003.

Wolff, Rebecca, and Jenette Nagy, "Section 6. Training for Conflict Resolution." http://ctb.ku.edu/en/table-of-contents/implement/provide-information-enhance-skills/conflict-resolution/main.

Wolters, Raymond. *The Burden of Brown: Thirty Years of School Desegregation*. Knoxville: University of Tennessee Press, 1992.

Yelle, Robert. *Semiotics of Religion: Signs of the Sacred in History*. London: Black, 2012.

Yoder, John Howard. *The Politics of Jesus*. Grand Rapids: Eerdmans, 1994.

Zehr, Howard. *The Little Book of Restorative Justice: Revised and Updated*. New York: Good, 2015.

Zehr, Howard, and Harry Mika. "Fundamental Concepts of Restorative Justice." *Contemporary Justice Review: Issues in Criminal, Social, and Restorative Justice* 1.1 (1997) 47–56.

Zorbas, Eugenia. "Reconciliation in Post-Genocide Rwanda," *African Journal of Legal Studies* 1.1 (2004) 29–52.

Index

Abimelech, 29
Abraham, 29–30, 39, 45
Abrahamic faiths, 45, 48, 94–95, 105–7, 110, 112, 116, 119–20
Acts 10, 15–16
Acts 17, 109
Adam and Eve, 9
African Americans, 19–22, 44
African and African American relationships, 19–22
African diaspora, 19–22
African National Congress (ANC), 42–43
Ahab, 30–31
Ahaz king of Judah, 83
American church culture, 33
American Dream, 43–44
American society, 43–44, 92, 113–14
Anabaptists, 104–5
ANC (African National Congress), 42–43
anger, 68–74
Antonine Plague, 53–54
apartheid, 41–43
Aram (Syria), 83
Areopagus, 109
asking for a drink from a Samaritan, 40

Assyrian empire, 83
asylum seekers, 32–33
attitude toward conflict, 113
Aurelius, Marcus, 53

Baal, 30–31
Babylon, 83
Baird N'Diaye, Diana, 21
Bethlehem, 106
biases, 26–27
Bible. *See* Scriptures
Big Island, 18
black America, 18–19, 22
Black Lives Matter movement, 74, 97
blackness, 18, 21
Bonhoeffer, Dietrich, 108
Bowles, Samuel, 48
Bowman, Carl, 104–5
Boys Brigade, 6–7

Cain and Abel, 10
California robbery story, 71
Canaan, 83
capitalism, 48–49
capricious God, 60–61
Center for Global Development, 56
Center for Nonviolence and Conflict Transformation (CNCT), 45–48, 94

Index

cheap grace, 108
Christianity
    and Abrahamic faiths, 112
    and discipleship, 100
    and hospitality, 28–29, 32–34
    and King, 118
    and listening, 66–67
    and peacemaking, 23, 65
    and reconciliation, 101
    and semiotic signs of building peace, 114–15
    and a shared mission, 107
churches and hospitality, 28–29, 32–33
Church of the Brethren, 104–5
Church of the Nativity, 106
Church World Service, 33
civic responsibilities, 67
Civil Rights Act of 1965, 95
Civil Rights movement, 45–47, 74, 92–93, 95
classism, 43–44, 48
CNCT (Center for Nonviolence and Conflict Transformation), 45–48, 94
collaboration, 57–58
colonialism, 18, 20–21, 41–42
common language, 118n30
community building, 46, 102, 105–8
community policing, 97–99
compassionate living, 120
conflict and peace, 23
conflict and violence, 119
conflict mediation, 117
conflict resolution, 100–102, 117
conflict transformation, 47–48, 64–65, 95–96, 106, 107, 113–18, 118n30, 119–20
conversion experience of Peter, 15
Copeland-Carson, Jacqueline, 20
Cornelius, 15–17, 26, 28
"The Cost of Discipleship" (Bonhoeffer), 108

COVID-19, 52–59
creative and constructive use of anger, 72–73
Cyrus the Persian, 83

Dayton, Ohio, 70
Delany, Martin, 20
democracy, 48
denunciation of idols, 85
desegregation, 91–94
discipleship, 100
discrimination, 64, 93
divine vocation, 12
Du Bois, W. E. B., 20

early Christians, 29, 33–34, 60
Edward, Brent Hayes, 20
Eliezer, 28–29
Elijah, 30–31, 88
embedded beliefs, 26–27
enemies, 27–28, 59–62, 89
Ephesians 2, 106
Ephesians 6:10–17, 22–23
Espinal, Edith, 33
evangelism, 9
evil, 46, 59, 63, 71
experiencing reality, 27

faith
    faith expressions, 112
    faith journey, 107–8
    faith language, 115–16
    and selflessness, 90–91
Falcon, Rabbi, 107
Fisk, Shannon, 92
Foreign Exchange (Forex), 69–70
forgiveness, 12, 67, 88
freedom, 48–49
friendliness, 27–28
fundamentalism, 109–10

Galan, 54
Gandhi, 109
gang-related violence, 34

Index

Garvey, Marcus, 20
gender-based violence, 56
Genesis 12, 39
Genesis 18:1–16, 30
Genesis 37:4, 62
gentiles, 15–17, 70
genuine hospitality, 27–28
geographic policing, 99
Gethsemane, 6, 10–12, 15, 89
gift-giving, 27
Gintis, Herbert, 48
globalization, 94, 110
God
    and Abraham, 39
    as capricious, 60–61
    grace of, 67
    and hospitality, 31–32
    and justice, 50
    and mountain metaphors, 87
    and suffering, 59
    as universal Judge, 82
Golden Rule, 95
gospel, 8–10, 11
grace, 108
Guder, Darrell, 28

Haruna, 7–9
Hawaii, 17–18
healing, 10, 12, 89–91
Hezekiah, 83
historic peace church, 104
Hopkins, Paul, 20
hospitality, 26–34
    of Abraham, 29–30
    and being polite, 27–28
    from a biblical perspective, 29–32
    in the church, 28–29
    and early Christians, 29, 33–34
    and Elijah, 30–31
    as a form of peacemaking, 26–27, 32–33
    genuine, 27–28
    radical expression of, 32–34
    and refuge, 29, 32–33
    untamed, 28–29
ICE (Immigration and Custom Enforcement), 32–33
idolatry, 30–31
"I Have a Dream" speech, 58–59
illnesses, 59
Iman Rahman, 107
immigrants, 21, 32–34
Immigration and Custom Enforcement (ICE), 32–33
immigration policy in the United States, 21
information gathering, 102
injustice, 49, 69–71, 74
inner-city youth, 34
intentionality, 28
interaction, 114
interfaith dialogue, 94–95, 108–12
internal violence of the spirit, 46
international communities, 57–58
Isaac, 29
Isaiah 2:1–5, 82–86
Isaiah 53, 65
Islam, 107, 112, 114–15
Israel, 39–40, 83
Italy, 53

James (disciple), 11, 88
Jensen, David, 47
Jeremiah, 61
Jesus
    in Bethlehem, 106
    capture of, 89–90
    cleansing of the temple, 68–71, 72–74
    and Gethsemane, 10–12
    and healing the aggressor, 12, 90–91
    and historical study, 107
    and hospitality, 33
    and interfaith dialogue, 110–11
    and Isaiah's prophecy, 84–85
    and Jewish culture, 16–17

Index

Jesus (continued)
   and justice, 49
   and King, 118
   and loving your enemies, 59–60
   and mountain metaphors, 87–88
   and the paths of the zealots, 14–15
   and Paul's description of the inner spiritual battle, 22–23
   and peacemaking, 6–10
   and radical obedience, 40–41
   and radical reconciliation, 106–7
   response to the Roman Empire, 65–66
   and righteous anger, 69–71
   in Samaria, 39–40
   transfiguration of, 88
   and violence, 12
Jesus and Nonviolence: A Third Way (Wink), 111
Jewish culture, 15–17
Jewish tradition, 65
John 3:30, 23
John 18:25–27, 11–12
John (disciple), 11, 69, 88, 89
John the Baptist, 23
Jos, Nigeria, 6
Joseph and his brothers, 61–63
journey towards reconciliation, 100, 114
Judah, 83
Judaism, 107, 112, 114–15
Judas Iscariot, 10–11, 89
justice, 46, 49–50, 58, 69

King, Martin Luther Jr., 23, 45–48, 49, 55, 58–59, 63, 90, 118
Kingian Nonviolence and Leadership Development, 95
Kingian Nonviolence for Law Enforcement, 97–98

Kingian nonviolence leadership development, 45–48
1 Kings 15:26, 30
1 Kings 17, 30–31
Klerk, F. W. de, 42
Konadu-Agyemang, Kwadwo, 20–21
Kouyaté, Tiemako Garan, 20

language of faith, 115–16
leadership development, 45–48
leadership in the faith community, 29, 64–65, 67
learned falsehoods, 26–27
Lederach, John Paul, 100, 114, 117–18, 118n30
"Letter from a Birmingham Jail" (King), 23
Leviticus 11, 16–17
listening, 66–67, 102
living sacrifices, 14
love, 71, 115
love of God, 41
loving your enemies, 27–28, 59–63, 89
Luke (disciple), 11–12, 33, 89

Mackenzie, Don, 107
Malchus, 6, 9–12
Mandela, Nelson, 42–43
Mark 11:15, 69
Mark (disciple), 11, 89
materialism, 49
Matthew 9:16–17, 96
Matthew 18, 100
Matthew (disciple), 11, 89, 118
Mauna Loa, 18
The Meaning and End of Religion (Smith), 114
messianic movements, 14
Messianic prophesies, 82–86
method of peacemaking, 65–67
Micah, 82
Micah 4:4, 86

Index

militarism, 49
minority communities, 52–53, 54–56, 64, 93
miracles, 12
monotheistic religions, 114
Moses, 88, 104
mountain metaphors, 84–85, 86–88, 104
Mount Zion, 82–83
Muhammad, 8
Muslim-Christian conflict, 6–8

Nigeria, 6–7, 17
9/11 attacks, 119
nonviolence, 34, 45–48, 55–57, 58, 65, 118
nonviolent policing, 98–99
Northern Kingdom, 83

officer residency program, 99
oneness, 120
openness, 66
orientation metaphor, 85

pandemics, 52–58
parables, 106
Paul (apostle), 22–23, 29, 69, 106, 109
peacemaking
    and Abrahamic faiths, 112, 116
    and the Center for Nonviolence and Conflict Transformation, 45
    and Christian approach, 65–67
    and conflict transformation, 64–65, 114–16, 119–20
    as core to Jesus' message, 6–10
    and the COVID-19 pandemic, 56–58
    vs. fighting back, 14
    and hospitality, 26–27, 32–33
    and interfaith dialogue, 95
    and the international community, 57–58
    and Isaiah's prophecy, 82–86
    method of, 65–67
    and mountain metaphors, 104
    and putting down your sword, 17, 22–23
    and reconciliation, 88, 100–102
    and the reign of the Messiah, 84
    and religious leaders, 64–65, 67
    and theological challenges, 23
Peel, Robert, 97
Peirce, C. S., 116
Pentateuch, 82
People Who Care, 64
People Who Care v. Rockford Board of Education School District #205, 92–93
personal peace with God, 23
Peter (disciple), 6, 11–12, 14–17, 22–24, 26, 28, 88
Pharisees, 89
Pietism movements, 104–5
plague, 53–54
plowshare metaphor, 85–86
policing, 19, 72, 97–99
policy of nations, 55
predatory policing, 19
problem solving, 102
prophesies, 82–86
proselytization, 45, 91, 95, 100
pruning-hook, 86
putting down your sword, 17–19, 21–23

racial diversity, 18–19
racial hierarchy, 18
racial inequality, 43–44, 64
racial profiling, 19, 72
racial segregation, 95
racism, 9–10, 19, 43–44, 49, 72, 92, 118
radical expression of hospitality, 32–34
radical obedience, 40–41

INDEX

radical peacemaking, 65
radical reconciliation, 106
reconciliation, 88, 99–102, 106, 118n30
reflection, 102
refuge, 29, 32–33
refugees, 32–34
Regional Historical Center, 93
reign of the Messiah, 84
religion
    and conflict resolution, 100–101, 114–16, 119–20
    and dialogues, 94–95
    and diversity, 110, 120
    and leaders, 29, 64–65, 67
    and symbols, 115–16
    and violence, 7–8
Reorganization Plan, 93
reorientation, 26–27
revolution of values, 49
righteous anger, 69–71
righteousness, 50
Rockford, Illinois, 18–19, 44, 63–65, 66–67, 91–94, 104–7, 109–10
Rockford Board of Education, 63–65
Rockford Partners for Excellence (RP4E), 105–7
Rockford School District (RSD), 92–94, 95–96
Roman Empire, 65–66
Rome, 53–54, 60
Rome, overthrow of, 14
RP4E (Rockford Partners for Excellence), 105–7
Ruskin, John, 41–42

sacrificial hospitality, 29–32
Samaria, 39–40
sanctuaries, 29, 32–33
sanctuary cities, 33
school desegregation, 91–94
Scriptures
    and hospitality, 27, 33
    and interfaith dialogue, 110–11
    and justice, 49–50
    and loving your enemies, 61–63
    and mountain metaphors, 87–88
    and religious dialogues, 94–95
    and violence, 7
    and a willingness to critique, 120
second conversion, 15
seekers, 109
self-defense, 6, 14, 23
selfishness, 90
selflessness, 90–91
semiotics
    defined, 112
    imagery, 84–85
    understanding, 115–17, 120
separation and suspicion, 111
Sermon on the Mount, 40, 59–60, 88, 118
shared experience, 120
shared mission, 105–8
sharing of food, 29
Shechem, 39
Sheikh Danjuma, 8
signs of conflict, 113–14
simple living, 120
Skinner, Elliott Percival, 21
slavery, 44
Smith, Wilfred Cantwell, 114
social media, 73
South Africa, 17, 41–43
Stride Toward Freedom (King), 45, 95
suffering, 46, 120
Sufism, 7–8
Supreme Court, 64, 92–94
symbols, 115–16
Syrian plow, 85–86
systemic inequality, 56
systemic racism, 43–44

Takyi, Baffour K., 20
temptation, 11
terrorism, 119–20
theological challenges and peacemaking, 23
theological semiotics, 115–16
Tiglath-Pileser, 83
trans-Atlantic slave trade, 20–21
transfiguration of Jesus, 88
Truth and Reconciliation Commission, 43
Tutu, Desmond, 99

ubuntu (humanness), 99
unclean animals, 16–17
United Nations, 49
unity, 96
untamed hospitality, 28–29
urbanization, 110
US District Court, 63–64

violence, 7–10, 14, 23, 34, 47–48, 56, 58, 119
Volney, Constantin-François, 85–86

war footing, 57
welcoming, 27–29
West Middle School (WMS), 64–65
white people, 44
White racial framing, 22
Wink, Walter, 111
Winnebago County, Illinois, 63–64
witnessing, 94

Yelle, Robert, 112

zealotry, 14–15

www.ingramcontent.com/pod-product-compliance
Lightning Source LLC
Chambersburg PA
CBHW051108160426
43193CB00010B/1358